Schweizer Grand Prix Design

Grand Prix suisse de design   Gran Premio svizzero di design

Swiss Grand Award for Design

2024

Schweizer Grand Prix Design 2024

Der Schweizer Grand Prix Design zeichnet exemplarische Karrieren aus und bietet Sichtbarkeit für die Designschaffenden, deren Arbeit in der Sparte besonders interessante Wege und Gedankengänge eröffnet.

Welchen Stimmen wollen wir in einer Welt voller Lärm Gehör verschaffen? Sollen wir diejenigen würdigen, deren Arbeit dazu dient, unsere Objekte, Plakate, Webseiten oder Kleider schöner zu gestalten? Diejenigen, die sie nachhaltiger machen? Diejenigen, die Design als sozialen Akt verstehen? Kann Design überhaupt neue Botschaften vermitteln? Was bedeuten Denken und Kreieren im Jahr 2024, wenn die Welt in ihrer ganzen Vielfalt und Komplexität berücksichtigt wird?

Die Jury pflegt einen lebendigen Austausch zu diesen Fragen und misst der Botschaft, die sie mit der Wahl der Preisträgerinnen und Preisträger sendet, grösste Bedeutung bei. Es geht darum, die Arbeit von Einzelpersonen auszuzeichnen, die einen neuartigen, kreativen, engagierten Ansatz zur Anwendung bringen oder die Disziplin bedeutend geprägt haben und weiterhin prägen – selbstverständlich ohne dabei die Frauen zu vergessen, die besonders in der Vergangenheit weniger sichtbar waren. Ein Preis des Bundes, der von Kolleginnen und Kollegen aus der Sparte vergeben wird, würdigt auch Designschaffende, die die Grenzen ihrer Praxis ausloten.

2024 fiel die Wahl auf Persönlichkeiten, die in ihren Bereichen neue Wege beschreiten. Der Beitrag von Paola De Martin geht weit über die traditionelle Forschung hinaus. Mit ihren kritischen Betrachtungen bietet sie eine transdisziplinäre Herangehensweise an das Design, das sie in den gesellschaftlichen und politischen Kontext setzt. Bei ihr werden die Themen von Migration, Rassismus und gesellschaftlichem Ausschluss innerhalb der Disziplin betrachtet. Die Modedesignerin Lucie Meier hat in beeindruckender Geschwindigkeit international Karriere gemacht. Mit 40 Jahren arbeitet sie für grosse Häuser wie Louis Vuitton, Balenciaga, Dior oder Jil Sander. Wer seine Karriere im Ausland macht, erhält in der Schweiz oft spät Anerkennung. Mit Lucie Meier wollen wir eine Designerin würdigen, die über sichere und feine Kenntnisse ihres Handwerks verfügt. Luciano Rigolini hat mit seinen 74 Jahren nie damit aufgehört, die Bilder zu hinterfragen. Durch den Akt der Aneignung erforscht er sein Material und interessiert sich dabei besonders für triviale Fotografien, die unter seinem Blick neues plastisches Potenzial entfalten. Gleichzeitig verfolgte er eine internationale Karriere als Produzent von dokumentarischen Autorenfilmen.

Indem sie mit dem Schweizer Grand Prix Design 2024 Persönlichkeiten würdigt, die sich an unterschiedlichen Momenten ihres Berufslebens befinden und die alle ihren ganz eigenen Ansatz verfolgen, zeigt die Jury die vielen Perspektiven, die das Design eröffnet. Die Anerkennung für so verschiedene

Arbeitsweisen wie die von Paola De Martin, Lucie Meier und Luciano Rigolini unterstreicht die Vielfalt der möglichen Karrieren. Mit ihrer persönlichen Geschichte beweisen sie, dass es nicht nötig ist, einer Elite anzugehören, um Anerkennung zu erlangen. Denn die Grundsteine ihrer Kreativität sind Reflexion und Engagement.

Nathalie Herschdorfer, Präsidentin der Eidgenössischen Designkommission

Einleitung

Auch 18 Jahre nach der Lancierung der «höchsten Auszeichnung des Schweizer Designs» ist der Schweizer Grand Prix Design für das Bundesamt für Kultur (BAK) ein hervorragendes Instrument, um die Breite beruflicher Entwicklungswege und die Vielfalt im Design aufzuzeigen. Durch die Anerkennung unterschiedlicher Perspektiven und Herangehensweisen wird unser Blick auf die Bedeutung von Design in unserer Gesellschaft jedes Jahr reicher und dynamischer.

Der Preis wurde 2007 erstmals vergeben. Kurz davor wurden im BAK die «Projektbeiträge Design» eingestellt und die Eidgenössische Designkommission (EDnK) suchte nach neuen Wegen, die Designerinnen und Designer gezielter und proaktiver mit Fördergeldern zu unterstützen.

Im ersten Jahr wurden auf Vorschlag der EDnK fünf Preise vergeben, die von Beginn an mit je 40 000 Franken dotiert waren. Mit dem bedeutenden Schriftgestalter Adrian Frutiger und mit Bernhard Schobinger, einem der einflussreichsten Schmuckkünstler Europas, wurden international renommierte Persönlichkeiten ausgezeichnet. Mit der 1991 gegründeten Designagentur Nose, der Modedesignerin Ruth Grüninger und dem Grafiker Cornel Windlin, damals knapp 40-jährig, kam zudem eine jüngere Generation zum Zug. Ziel des BAK war es, Designschaffenden zu ermöglichen, an innovativen Projekten zu arbeiten und ihr kreatives Potenzial weiterzuentwickeln, ohne sich ausschliesslich auf den kommerziellen Erfolg konzentrieren zu müssen.

Die Auszeichnungen prägen ein Stück Schweizer Designgeschichte. Die dazu erscheinende Publikation beinhaltet oftmals erste Sichtungen von Archiven und dient als Basis für künftige Werkpräsentationen und Forschungsarbeiten. Gerade im vergangenen Jahr bekamen zahlreiche ehemalige Preisträgerinnen des Schweizer Grand Prix Design (SGPD) eine eigene Plattform: Im Landesmuseum war eine monografische Ausstellung über das Ausnahmetalent im Schweizer Modedesign Ursula Rodel (SGPD 2009) zu entdecken. Über die Leuchtendesign-Pionierin Rosmarie Baltensweiler (2019) erschien im letzten September ein umfangreicher Werkkatalog, Eleonore Peduzzi Riva (2023), die weit mehr als das weltberühmte DS-600-Sofa mitentwickelt hat, wurde an Panels eingeladen und mehrfach interviewt, im Museum für Gestaltung Zürich konnte man jüngst die textilen Wunderwerke von Claudia Caviezel (2016) geniessen und Sarah Kueng und Lovis Caputo (2020) erhielten Ende 2023 den wohlverdienten Goldenen Hasen von Hochparterre. Und aktuell freuen wir uns über eine Publikation mit zwölf neuen Alphabeten von Rosmarie Tissi (2018), die im Verlag About Books erscheint.

Die diesjährigen Preisträgerinnen Paola De Martin und Lucie Meier sowie den Preisträger Luciano Rigolini verbindet die Fähigkeit, Traditionen zu hinterfragen und neue Wege zu beschreiten. Wie die drei mit ihrem innovativen Schaffen dazu beitragen, Vielfalt, Inklusion, Ethik, Zusammenarbeit und Technologie in der Kultur zu fördern, können Sie, liebe Leserin, lieber Leser, nun bei der Lektüre erfahren. Ich wünsche Ihnen viele spannende Entdeckungen und wie jedes Jahr auch viel Inspiration für Ihre eigenen Projekte.

Anna Niederhäuser
Leitung Design
Bundesamt für Kultur

Grand Prix suisse de design 2024

Le Grand Prix suisse de design distingue des carrières exemplaires et offre une visibilité à des créatrices et des créateurs dont le travail ouvre une voie ou des réflexions particulièrement intéressantes dans ce domaine.

Quelles voix faire entendre dans un monde aussi bruyant que le nôtre ? Faut-il valoriser celles et ceux qui conçoivent des créations destinées à rendre nos objets, nos affiches, nos sites Internet, nos vêtements plus beaux ? Celles et ceux qui les rendent plus durables ? Celles et ceux qui voient dans le design un acte social ? Le design peut-il être porteur de nouveaux messages ? Que signifie, en 2024, penser et créer tout en tenant compte de la diversité et de la complexité de notre monde ?

Le jury échange activement autour de ces questions et considère avec la plus grande attention le message qu'il souhaite transmettre en distinguant trois lauréat-e-s. Il s'agit de valoriser le travail d'individus à l'approche novatrice, créatrice ou engagée, ou encore qui exercent ou qui ont exercé une influence marquante dans leur discipline. Ceci, bien sûr, sans oublier les femmes, qui dans le passé ont souvent été reléguées à l'arrière plan. L'annonce des Grands Prix attire l'attention des médias et permet de parler des différents domaines du design à un public varié. Un prix fédéral, décerné par des pairs, rend aussi hommage à des professionnels qui explorent les contours de leur pratique.

En 2024, le choix s'est porté sur des personnes qui ont choisi un chemin novateur dans leur domaine. La contribution de Paola De Martin dépasse largement la recherche traditionnelle. Par ses réflexions critiques, elle offre une approche transdisciplinaire au design qu'elle intègre dans un contexte social et politique. Chez elle, les questions de migration, de racisme et d'exclusion sociale s'invitent dans la discipline. La créatrice de mode Lucie Meier mène une carrière internationale fulgurante. À 40 ans, elle a travaillé pour de grandes maisons, parmi lesquelles Louis Vuitton, Balenciaga, Dior et Jil Sander. Pour celles et ceux qui développent une carrière à l'étranger, la reconnaissance arrive souvent de façon tardive. Avec Lucie Meier, il s'agit de valoriser une créatrice qui a de solides et sensibles connaissances dans son métier. Enfin, Luciano Rigolini est à 74 ans un créateur qui n'a jamais cessé d'interroger les images. C'est par l'acte d'appropriation qu'il explore sa matière, s'intéressant particulièrement aux photographies vernaculaires. Sous son regard, les photographies dévoilent de nouvelles potentialités plastiques. En parallèle il a mené une carrière internationale comme producteur dans le domaine du film documentaire d'auteur.

En réunissant autour du Grand Prix suisse de design 2024, des individus se trouvant à différents moments de leur vie professionnelle et qui témoignent chacun-e d'une approche singulière, le jury signifie que le design ouvre de nombreuses perspectives. Reconnaître le travail de Paola De Martin, de Lucie

Meier et de Luciano Rigolini dont les pratiques sont relativement éloignées l'une de l'autre, permet de montrer des voies multiples. À travers leur histoire personnelle, on voit qu'il n'est pas nécessaire d'appartenir à une élite pour aspirer à la reconnaissance, car le ciment de leur créativité réside dans la réflexion et l'engagement.

Nathalie Herschdorfer, Présidente de la Commission fédérale de design

Introduction

Dix-huit ans après la création de la « plus prestigieuse distinction du design suisse », le Grand Prix suisse de design de l'Office fédéral de la culture (OFC) demeure un remarquable instrument qui permet de mettre en évidence la diversité du design et celle des parcours professionnels dans le domaine. En reconnaissant des perspectives et des approches différentes, nous pouvons d'année en année porter un regard de plus en plus riche et dynamique sur l'importance du design dans notre société.

C'est en 2007 que le prix a été décerné pour la première fois. Peu de temps auparavant, l'OFC avait cessé d'octroyer ses « contributions à des projets de design » et la Commission fédérale de design était à la recherche de nouvelles manières de soutenir les designers par des aides ciblées et proactives.

La première année, cinq prix ont été décernés sur proposition de la CFD ; comme aujourd'hui, chacun d'eux était doté d'une somme de 40 000 francs. Ils couronnaient, d'une part, des personnalités de renommée internationale, comme Adrian Frutiger, important créateur de caractères d'imprimerie, et Bernhard Schobinger, un des plus influents bijoutiers d'art d'Europe. Mais ils faisaient aussi une place à la nouvelle génération, avec l'agence de design Nose, fondée en 1991, la créatrice de mode Ruth Grüninger et le graphiste Cornel Windlin, alors tout juste quarantenaire. Le but de l'OFC était de permettre à des designers de travailler à des projets novateurs et de développer leurs potentialités créatives sans qu'ils soient contraints de se concentrer sur le succès commercial.

Les prix décernés sont le reflet de tout un pan de l'histoire du design suisse. Souvent, la publication qui les accompagne donne un aperçu des archives des lauréats qui sera un point de départ pour des rétrospectives et des travaux de recherche ultérieurs. L'année dernière, nombre d'anciens lauréats du Grand Prix suisse de design ont été mis sur le devant de la scène. Le Musée national suisse a ainsi consacré une exposition monographique à Ursula Rodel (Grand Prix 2009), créatrice de mode d'un exceptionnel talent, tandis qu'un riche catalogue de l'œuvre de Rosmarie Baltensweiler (2019), pionnière du design de luminaires, paraissait en septembre dernier. Dans le même temps, Eleonore Peduzzi Riva (2023), dont le canapé DS-600, mondialement connu, n'est de loin pas la seule création, courait les tables rondes et les entretiens, et le Musée du design de Zurich accueillait les merveilleuses œuvres textiles de Claudia Caviezel (2016), alors que la revue Hochparterre attribuait à Sarah Kueng et Lovis Caputo (2020) une distinction amplement méritée, le Goldener Hase, et que, tout récemment, nous pouvions nous réjouir de la parution aux éditions About Books de douze nouveaux alphabets de Rosmarie Tissi (2018).

Les deux lauréates et le lauréat de cette année, Paola De Martin, Lucie Meier et Luciano Rigolini, s'apparentent par leur capacité de remettre en question les traditions et de s'engager dans de nouvelles voies. Dans les pages qui suivent, vous apprendrez comment ces trois créateurs innovants promeuvent une culture basée sur la diversité, l'inclusion, l'éthique, la coopération et la technologie. Je vous souhaite de faire des découvertes captivantes et d'y puiser, comme chaque année, une riche inspiration pour vos propres projets.

Anna Niederhäuser
Responsable design
Office fédéral de la culture

[IT → p. 43, EN → p. 45]

Lucie Meier

Lucie Meier   Durch Instinkt

von Christiane Arp

Wenn sie sich auf anderem Weg kreativ ausdrücken wollte als mit Modedesign, würde sie das nicht mit Worten tun, sagt sie. Dabei reichen ihr nur wenige Worte, um ihr Innerstes zu offenbaren. Ein einziges ist genug auf die Frage nach einem Beispiel für perfektes Design: «die Natur». Eine Antwort, die beim Gegenüber sofort ein Kopfkino in Gang setzt und den kreativen Kosmos von Lucie Meier ausleuchtet. Es ist keine romantische Verklärung, sondern eine Art intuitiver Dialog, der nach einer Stoff werdenden, gestalterischen natürlichen Lösung strebt – ursprünglich in Gang gesetzt durch die Inspiration von einem Kunstwerk, einem Buch, vielleicht auch einem Gefühl, «einem Moment in meinem Leben». Was sie daraus seit nunmehr sieben Jahren gemeinsam mit ihrem Mann Luke als kreatives Duo für Jil Sander entstehen lässt, setzt neue ästhetische aber auch ethische Massstäbe in der Modebranche. «Evolution in Progress», umschreibt sie ihren kreativen Prozess. Neues nur der Neuheit willen zu schaffen, ist ihr zuwider. «Alles, was wir kreieren, muss einen Sinn haben, muss uns berühren».

Dieses haptische wie emotionale Berühren durch Kleidung faszinierte sie von klein auf. Aufgewachsen als Lucie Mennig am Fusse des Matterhorns, in Zermatt, wo die Familie – erst die Eltern, nun der Bruder mit seiner Frau – bis heute das Restaurant «Zum See» in einem mehr als 500 Jahre alten Chalet betreibt, wusste Lucie Meier schon sehr früh, dass sie einmal etwas mit Mode machen wolle. Auslöser war ihre Mutter, die Stoffe und Mode liebt. Und besonders Jil Sander.

Die ersten eigenen Schritte in die Modewelt führten sie dann an die Polimoda nach Florenz, wo sie begann, Modemarketing zu studieren. Ein kurzer Ausflug, der ihr schnell klar machte, dass dieser Bereich der Fashionwelt nicht ihrer Sehnsucht entspricht. Der Stopover an der italienischen Hochschule ist dennoch richtungsweisend für ihr Leben. Denn sie lernt einen jungen Kanadier mit Schweizer Wurzeln kennen und lieben: Luke Meier. Sie gehen gemeinsam nach New York und Lucie beginnt für das Magazin *Nylon* zu arbeiten. Sie beschliesst, Modedesign zu studieren und bewirbt sich an der École de la Chambre Syndicale in Paris. Anschliessend fängt sie als Praktikantin bei Louis Vuitton unter Marc Jacobs an. «Eine unglaubliche Erfahrung», wie sie sagt, die zu einem fünfjährigen Engagement im Team des genialischen Modevisionärs wurde. Die nächste Station nicht weniger hochkarätig: Bei Balenciaga kreiert sie mit Nicolas Ghesquière die Showkollektion des legendären Labels. Ein Wechselbad kreativen Genies: «Bei Marc Jacobs entstand eine Kollektion in drei Wochen, bei Nicolas Ghesquière nahmen wir uns sechs Monate Zeit». Schliesslich folgt Dior, wo sie zur Headdesignerin des Sommerteams unter Raf Simons avanciert. Nach dessen Weggang Ende 2015 leitet sie interimistisch mit Serge Ruffieux das Couture-Haus, bis Maria Grazia Chiuri 2016 die Führung übernahm.

Der Ruf an die kreative Spitze von Jil Sander 2017 erwies sich – «früher als gedacht» – als erfüllter Wunsch: Neben dem Lieblingslabel aus der Kindheit auch in Form der Zusammenarbeit mit ihrem Mann. So unterschiedlicher die berufliche Herkunft der beiden nicht sein könnte, erweist sich das Teamwork rasch als kongenial. Lucie, die intuitiv aus dem Bauch heraus kreiert auf der einen, Luke, der leidenschaftlich analysiert und Prozesse erforscht, auf der anderen Seite. Er bewundert in der Zusammenarbeit «ihre Ruhe, ihre Intuition und ihr absolut unfehlbares fotografisches Gedächtnis». Gemeinsam suchen sie nach Wegen, Mode Sinn und Schönheit zu verleihen, in einer Zeit, in der das klassische Schubladendenken zwischen Opulenz und Minimalismus ad absurdum geführt wird. Etwas, das die Spannung, die durch Gegensätze entsteht, befeuert. Nach kreativer Essenz.

In der selbstgefälligen, um jeden Preis Aufsehen erregenden Modewelt ist Lucie Meier eine Ausnahmeerscheinung, die gerade deshalb gesehen und gehört wird, weil sie in sich ruhend einen nachhaltigen kreativen Weg gefunden hat, den viele andere noch hektisch suchen.

Dabei geht es auch viel um neue Materialien, die Umsetzung und Überprüfbarkeit nachhaltiger Prozesse, um zeitgemässe Linien, die das Gen der Zeitlosigkeit in sich tragen. «Wir alle haben die Schränke voll mit Kleidern», sagt Lucie Meier. «Es ist nicht so, dass jemand unbedingt einen neuen Mantel bräuchte. Man braucht jedoch etwas, das einen berührt und bewegt. Ich hoffe, dass ich den Leuten etwas Gutes geben kann, und versuche, Menschen den Alltag zu verbessern oder zu erleichtern, wenn ich zu ihrem Selbstvertrauen etwas beitragen kann.»

Christiane Arp war von 2003 bis 2020 Chefredakteurin der deutschen VOGUE. Die studierte Modedesignerin ist Gründungsmitglied und Vorstandsvorsitzende des Fashion Council Germany. Sie gilt als eine der wichtigsten Nachwuchsförderinnen junger Designtalente und kennt Lucie Meier und ihren Mann seit vielen Jahren.

Lucie Meier À l'instinct

par Christiane Arp

Si elle voulait exprimer sa créativité par d'autres moyens que la mode, ce ne serait pas par le verbe, dit-elle. Pourtant, il lui suffit de quelques mots pour révéler ce qu'elle a de plus intime. Si on lui demande de citer un exemple de design parfait, elle répond en un mot : « la nature ». Ce qui pousse immédiatement l'interlocuteur à se faire une image mentale et éclaire le cosmos créatif de Lucie Meier. Nulle transfiguration romantique dans ce processus, plutôt une sorte de dialogue intuitif qui s'efforce de trouver une solution formelle naturelle appelée à se transformer en matière – sur une inspiration insufflée à l'origine par une œuvre d'art, un livre, peut-être aussi un sentiment, « un moment dans ma vie ». Ce qui en résulte depuis sept ans pour la marque Jil Sander, où elle forme avec son mari Luke un duo créatif, redéfinit les codes de l'esthétique, mais impose aussi de nouveaux critères éthiques dans le secteur de la mode. « Evolution in progress » : c'est par cette formule qu'elle décrit son processus créatif. La nouveauté pour la nouveauté la rebute. « Tout ce que nous créons doit avoir un sens, doit nous toucher. »

Enfant, elle était déjà fascinée par ce contact, aussi bien haptique qu'émotionnel, instauré par le vêtement. Lucie Meier, née Mennig, a grandi au pied du Cervin, à Zermatt, où sa famille – autrefois ses parents, aujourd'hui son frère et sa femme – tient le restaurant « Zum See » dans un chalet de plus de cinq siècles, et elle a su très tôt qu'un jour, elle ferait quelque chose dans la mode. Une vocation suscitée par sa mère, qui aimait les étoffes et la mode. Et particulièrement Jil Sander.

Ses premiers pas dans le monde de la mode la mènent à l'école Polimoda de Florence, où elle commence à étudier le marketing. Un bref passage, qui lui fait vite comprendre que cet aspect de l'univers fashion ne correspond pas à son désir. Son escale dans l'école italienne aura pourtant une influence décisive sur sa vie. Elle y fait la connaissance d'un jeune Canadien aux racines suisses, Luke Meier, qui deviendra quelques années plus tard son mari. Ensemble, ils partent à New York, et Lucie commence à travailler pour le magazine *Nylon*. Elle décide de faire des études de stylisme et pose sa candidature à l'École de la Chambre Syndicale de la Couture Parisienne. Diplôme en poche, elle débute comme stagiaire chez Louis Vuitton, où officie alors Marc Jacobs. « Une expérience incroyable », dit-elle, qu'elle poursuivra en restant cinq ans dans l'équipe de ce génie visionnaire. Étape suivante, non moins prestigieuse : chez Balenciaga, elle imagine avec Nicolas Ghesquière les collections de la maison parisienne. Deux formes quasi opposées de génie créatif : « Avec Marc Jacobs, une collection était créée en trois semaines, avec Nicolas Ghesquière, nous prenions six mois. » Vient ensuite Dior, où elle est promue « head designer » de la collection été sous Raf Simons. Au départ de celui-ci, fin 2015, elle assure la direction par intérim du studio de haute couture et de prêt-à-porter aux côtés de Serge Ruffieux, jusqu'à la nomination de Maria Grazia Chiuri en 2016.

En 2017, quand elle est appelée à la direction artistique de Jil Sander, c'est un vœu qui se réalise (« plus tôt que prévu ») : non seulement c'est la marque fétiche de son enfance, mais de plus, elle va collaborer avec son mari. Leurs origines professionnelles ont beau n'avoir rien en commun, l'association de ce tandem fait rapidement des étincelles. D'un côté Lucie, qui crée à l'instinct, et de l'autre Luke, qui adore analyser et disséquer des processus. Dans cette collaboration, il admire « son calme, son intuition, et sa mémoire photographique absolument infaillible ». Ensemble, ils cherchent des moyens de donner du sens et de la beauté à la mode, à une époque où la dichotomie classique entre opulence et minimalisme tourne à l'absurde. Quelque chose qui attise la tension née des contraires. L'essence de la créativité.

Dans la mode, univers complaisant en quête de buzz à tout prix, Lucie Meier fait figure d'exception, elle qui est vue et entendue précisément parce qu'elle a trouvé, stable et tranquille, une voie créative durable que bien d'autres continuent à chercher frénétiquement.

Il est aussi beaucoup question de nouvelles matières, de processus durables à mettre en œuvre et à contrôler, de lignes contemporaines porteuses du gène de l'intemporalité. « Nous avons tous des placards pleins à craquer », dit Lucie Meier. « Ce n'est pas comme si nous avions impérativement besoin d'un nouveau manteau. Mais il nous faut quelque chose qui nous touche et nous émeuve. J'espère pouvoir offrir aux gens quelque chose de bon, et j'essaie d'améliorer ou de faciliter leur quotidien en leur donnant un peu plus confiance en eux. »

Christiane Arp a été rédactrice en chef du VOGUE allemand de 2003 à 2020. Styliste de formation, elle a été membre fondatrice et présidente du conseil d'administration du Fashion Council Germany. Elle est considérée comme une actrice essentielle de la promotion des jeunes talents et connaît Lucie Meier et son mari depuis de nombreuses années.

[IT → p. 37, EN → p. 38]

A

D, E

A. Spring/Summer 2024 Collection documented by Jack Davison. Photo © Jack Davison
B. Spring/Summer 2024 Collection documented by Jack Davison. Photo © Jack Davison
C. Jolie documented by Mario Sorrenti at UNESCO World Heritage Site Mallorca, Spain, September 2017. Photo © Mario Sorrenti
D. Spring/Summer 2022 Collection documented by Chris Rhodes. Photo © Chris Rhodes
E. Fall/Winter 2023 Collection documented by Chris Rhodes. Photo © Chris Rhodes
F. ARC'TERYX × JIL SANDER+ Collaboration, Fall/Winter 2021. Video still © Stephen Kidd
G. Prefall 2020 Collection, Milan, Italy, November 2019. Photo © Tim El Kaïm
H. The Fall/Winter 2020 Campaign project Mai Edström documented by Anders Edström. Photo © Anders Edström
I. Amanda and Evon, Apple Eaters, October 2012. Photo © Estate of Larry Fink
J. Women's and men's Spring/Summer 2023 show. Photo © Thomas Mailaender
K. Fall/Winter 2023 Collection documented by Chris Rhodes. Photo © Chris Rhodes
L. Jolie and Sofia backstage at Fall/Winter 2018 show, Milan, Italy. Photo © Lina Scheynius

[DE] CHRISTIANE ARP IM GESPRÄCH MIT LUCIE MEIER, 17. JANUAR 2024

Christiane Arp: Machst Du denn eigentlich einen Unterschied zwischen Kleidung und Mode?
Lucie Meier: Auf jeden Fall. Die Funktion von Kleidung ist es, den Körper zu beschützen – vor Kälte oder Hitze, der Sonne, Scham… Mode ist viel mehr. Ein Objekt der Fiktion, der Emotionen, eine Reflexion der Zeit.
CA: Auch Kunst?
LM: Nicht *Fine Art*, aber angewandte Kunst. Ich würde sagen, sie ist ein Medium der Expression. Für mich, aber natürlich auch für den Menschen, der sie trägt. Man kann damit etwas über sich erzählen – oder auch etwas verstecken. Je nachdem, was man gerade trägt, verwandelt man sich vielleicht auch ein Stück weit.
CA: Waren Mode und Design schon immer die Sprache, mit der Du Dich ausdrücken wolltest, könntest Du Dir auch einen anderen kreativen Bereich vorstellen?
LM: Also sicher nicht mit Worten. Das ist nicht meine Stärke. Ich wusste schon sehr früh, dass ich etwas mit Mode machen möchte. Das war aber zuerst eher so ein Gefühl, ohne dass ich wirklich Bescheid wusste. Ich habe dann ja auch zuerst Modemarketing studiert, bevor ich mich fürs Design entschied. Ich könnte mir auch vorstellen, mich mit Architektur auszudrücken – mit Räumen. Aber Mode ist für mich das natürlichste Ausdrucksmittel.
CA: Du nennst unter anderem Donald Judd, John Chamberlain, Wolfgang Tillmanns und John Pawson als Inspirationsquellen. Machst Du eigentlich einen Unterschied zwischen Vorbild, Inspiration und Einfluss?
LM: Ein Vorbild ist jemand, den ich in meinem Leben habe, der einen positiven Einfluss darauf hat. Jemand, den ich persönlich kenne. Inspiration und auch Einfluss sind etwas von Menschen, deren Werk ich bewundere, die ich aber vielleicht gar nicht persönlich kenne. Das Werk von einem Künstler oder einer Designerin wie Rei Kawakubo beispielsweise oder Ed Ruscha. Wenn jemand über so viele Jahre so tolle Arbeiten macht, dann beeindruckt mich das sehr und inspiriert mich.
CA: Stimmt es, dass bei Dir immer ein Künstler, eine Künstlerin oder ein Kunstwerk der Ausgangspunkt einer neuen Kollektion ist?

1. Lucie and Luke Meier portrait. Photo © Jack Davison

«Was brauche ich heute, was berührt mich, was beeinflusst mich? Darum geht es.»

LM: Nicht immer, aber sehr oft ist dies der Fall. Das kann auch ein Gefühl sein oder ein Buch oder ein ganz bestimmter Moment in unserem Leben.
CA: Und wenn Du diesen Startpunkt gefunden hast, startet dann zuerst der Dialog mit Deinem Mann, bevor ihr diese Idee ins Atelier zu Euren Mitarbeitenden tragt?
LM: Ja, es beginnt immer mit einer Diskussion zwischen mir und Luke. Dann machen wir ein Dossier mit Inspirationen, teilen einige Bücher, Kleidungsstücke und Objekte mit unserem Team und der Ball kommt sozusagen ins Rollen, wird durch weitere Recherchen immer präziser und konkreter.

Christiane Arp: Do you actually make a distinction between clothing and fashion?
Lucie Meier: Absolutely. The function of clothing is to protect the body – from cold or heat, the sun, shame... Fashion is much more than that: an object of fiction, of emotions, a reflection of the times.
CA: Art too?
LM: Not fine art, but applied art. I would say it's a medium of expression, not just for me, but of course also for the person who wears it. You can use fashion to tell something about yourself – or hide it. What you're wearing at any given moment might even transform you a little.

"What do I need today, what touches me, what influences me? That's what it's all about."

CA: Has fashion and design always been the language you wanted to express yourself with, or could you also imagine working in another creative field?
LM: Definitely not with words. That's not my strength. I knew from a very early age that I wanted to work in fashion one way or another, but it started as more of a feeling, without me really knowing. I first studied fashion marketing before I decided to go into design. I could also imagine expressing myself through architecture – with spaces. But for me, fashion is the most natural means of expression.
CA: You name, among others, Donald Judd, John Chamberlain, Wolfgang Tillmanns and John Pawson as sources of inspiration. Do you see any difference between role model, inspiration and influence?
LM: A role model is someone I have in my life who has a positive influence on it. Someone I know personally. Inspiration and influence come from people whose work I admire, even though I might not know them personally. Artists and designers such as Rei Kawakubo and Ed Ruscha are good examples. When someone does such great work for so many years, it really impresses me and inspires me.
CA: Is it true that you always take an artist or a work of art as the starting point for a new collection?
LM: That's not always the case, but very often. It can also be a feeling or a book or a very specific moment in our lives.
CA: Once you have found this starting point, do you start a dialogue with your husband before you take this idea to your colleagues in the studio?
LM: Yes, it always starts with a discussion between Luke and myself. Then we create a dossier with inspiration, share some books, items of clothing and objects with our team, and the ball starts rolling, so to speak, becoming more and more precise and concrete through further research.
CA: When you both started at Jil Sander in 2017, did you have anything like a master plan?
LM: Not really, but we felt confident in what we wanted to do because Jil Sander has always been very close to us as a brand. Intuitively, it was clear to us which direction we would take.
CA: Jil Sander has been given many nicknames and epithets: "queen of less", "queen of pure", minimalist... How would you describe Jil Sander? Do you identify your own work with such terms?

2. Jil Sander London Store.
Photo © Joss Mckinley

CA: Als ihr beide 2017 bei Jil Sander begonnen habt, gab es da so etwas wie einen Masterplan?

LM: Nicht wirklich. Aber dadurch, dass uns Jil Sander als Marke immer schon sehr nah war, fühlten wir uns sicher, in dem, was wir machen möchten. Intuitiv war uns klar, welche Richtung wir einschlagen werden.

CA: Jil Sander hat ja viele Namen und Attribute bekommen: «Queen of less», «Queen of pure», minimalistisch … Wie würdest Du Jil Sander beschreiben? Identifizierst Du Deine eigene Arbeit mit solchen Begriffen?

LM: Also nicht mit minimalistisch. Das ist nicht das richtige Wort. Ich finde, minimalistisch hat oft einen kalten Beigeschmack. Pur finde ich passender, denn da ist auch immer etwas sehr Humanes dabei – das ist die Essenz. Doch es beschreibt es nicht komplett. Jil Sander steht in meinen Augen für Modernität. Etwas Modernes kann durchaus auch sehr opulent sein.

CA: Vielleicht ist Einfachheit das treffendere Wort als pur? Die Suche nach der Essenz?

LM: Ja, durchaus! Etwas Opulentes kann einfach gestaltet sein – also nicht kompliziert – und umgekehrt. Das Material entscheidet am Ende auch ganz stark, wie wir etwas empfinden. Als wir Jil Sander getroffen haben, sagte sie: «Ich hoffe, ihr habt nichts von den Sachen, die ich kreiert

«Wir kreieren in einer autobiografischen Art und Weise. Wie und wo wir aufgewachsen sind, spielt da viel hinein.»

habe, noch in den Geschäften – es ist immer wichtig nach vorne zu schauen!» Das ist für uns auch enorm wichtig: der Kontext mit dem Jetzt. Was brauche ich heute, was berührt mich, was beeinflusst mich? Darum geht es.

CA: Jil Sander hat mal gesagt: «Ich mache nichts Neues um der Neuheit Willen.» Gilt das auch für Dich?

LM: Ich denke, alles, was ich kreiere, was wir kreieren, muss einen Sinn und Zusammenhang haben, muss uns berühren. Es ist eine *Evolution in Progress*.

CA: Gibt es einen Moment, an dem Du sagtest: «Ich bin angekommen bei Jil Sander»?

LM: Ich bin ja in Zermatt in den Bergen aufgewachsen, da gab es nicht wirklich viel Mode. Doch meine Mutter war, wenn man so sagen möchte, *Jil Sander-obsessed*. Und was die Kleidung mit ihr machte, wenn sie sie trug, war der eigentliche Grund, warum ich mich für Mode zu interessieren begann. Ich bin also schon vor vielen Jahren bei Jil Sander angekommen und fühlte mich der Marke nahe. Wenn es um eine erste essentielle Zufriedenheit mit dem Ergebnis unserer Arbeit geht, dann würde ich sagen, es war die Winter-Kollektion 2020, die wir kurz vor dem Lockdown präsentiert haben. Dafür war Pina Bausch die Inspiration. Doch auch jede Kollektion davor hat sich für uns gut angefühlt. Es war das Richtige in dem Moment.

CA: Ist es heute für den Erfolg einer Kollektion wichtig, dass man auch die Businessbereiche versteht. Oder blendest Du diesen Teil komplett aus?

LM: Es ist auf jeden Fall präsent. Aber ich denke, wir sind schon recht frei. Wenn man nur ans Business denkt im Designprozess, ist das nicht Sinn der Sache. Weil dabei geht es vor allem um Emotionen. Von daher kann man sich nicht nur damit befassen. Es ist sicher anders heute als in Zeiten, in denen ein Designjob nur Kreieren bedeutete. Ob man als Designer jedoch unbedingt eine Businessausbildung braucht, lasse ich dahingestellt. Auf jeden Fall ist der Job heute viel komplexer. Ich habe das Glück, dass Luke der Finanzexperte ist. Ich bin zwar bei jedem Meeting dabei, doch er hat in diesem Punkt wesentlich mehr Erfahrung als ich.

CA: Da sind wir beim Thema Arbeitsteilung. Trefft ihr alle Entscheidungen gemeinsam? Ohne Kompromisse?

LM: Zum Glück verstehen wir uns so gut, dass wir – fast – immer gleicher Meinung sind. Manche Leute fragen: «Wie könnt Ihr überhaupt zusammen arbeiten?» Ich kenne es aber gar nicht anders. Meine Eltern haben auch immer zusammen gearbeitet. Ich finde das eine tolle Sache. Kompromisse müssen wir eigentlich keine machen. Wenn wir mal geteilter Meinung sind, vertraut der eine dem anderen schlussendlich. Der Vorteil ist, dass wir das gleiche Interesse verfolgen und deswegen auch immer ehrlich zueinander sein können. Ich empfinde das als Bereicherung.

CA: Ihr seid seit 17 Jahren verheiratet. War es immer schon euer Wunsch auch zusammenzuarbeiten?

LM: Ja, wir hatten immer schon darüber gesprochen. Es ist schneller gekommen, als wir es erwartet haben. Wir wollten etwas zusammen machen. Was genau oder wie, das haben wir nie konkretisiert, aber es war unser Wunsch.

CA: Addiert ihr euch denn? Eure berufliche Herkunft könnte auf den ersten Blick nicht unterschiedlicher sein: Du mit Stationen bei Louis Vuitton, Balenciaga und Dior; Luke mit Supreme und OAMC.

LM: Sicher haben wir unterschiedliche Erfahrungen. Schlussendlich ist es aber nicht so verschieden, wie es manche vielleicht sehen. Weil unsere Herangehensweise ans Designen gleich ist. Wir kreieren in einer autobiografischen Art und Weise. Wie und wo wir aufgewachsen sind, spielt da viel hinein. Ich in der Enge der Schweizer Berge, wo die Welt gewissermassen zu mir kam. Luke

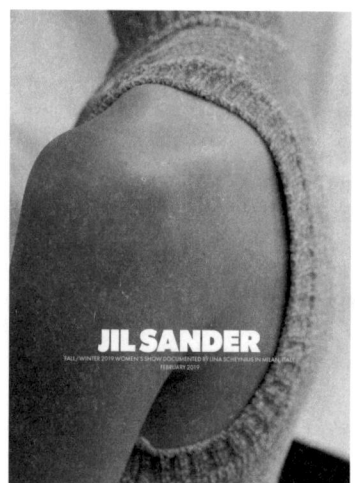

3. Fall/Winter 2019 women's show backstage.
Photo © Lina Scheynius

LM: Not minimalist, no. That's not the right word. I think minimalist often has a cold aftertaste. I think pure is more suitable because there's always something very human about it – that's the essence. But it doesn't describe it completely. In my eyes, Jil Sander represents modernity. Something modern can also be very opulent.

CA: Maybe simplicity is a better word than pure? The search for the essence?

LM: Yes, definitely! Something opulent can be simple in design – meaning not complicated – and vice versa. In the end, the material also plays a big part in determining how we feel about something. When we met Jil Sander, she said: "I hope you don't still have any of the things I created in the shops – it's always important to look forward!" That's also hugely important for us, staying in the here and now. What do I need today, what touches me, what influences me? That's what it's all about.

CA: Jil Sander once said "I don't do anything new for the sake of being new." Does that apply to you too?

LM: I think everything I create, everything we create, must have meaning and context, must touch us. It's an evolution in progress.

CA: Was there a moment when you thought, "I have arrived at Jil Sander"?

LM: I grew up in the mountains in Zermatt, where there wasn't really much fashion, but you could say my mother was obsessed with Jil Sander. What the clothes did to her when she wore them was the real reason I became interested in fashion. So I arrived at Jil Sander many years ago and felt close to the brand. As regards that first essential satisfaction with the result of our work, I'd say it was the winter 2020 collection that we presented shortly before the lockdown. Pina Bausch was the inspiration for this. But every collection before that also felt good to us. It was the right thing to do at that moment.

CA: Does the success of a collection hinge on understanding the business these days, or do you just block that out completely?

LM: It's definitely a factor, but I think we're quite free. If you only think about business in the design process, you're missing the point. It's all about emotions. So you can't just deal with that side of things. It is certainly different today than in times when a design job only meant creating,

4. Women's Fall/Winter 2020 show preparation documented by Larry Fink. Photo © Larry Fink

"We create in an autobiographical way. How and where we grew up plays a very important part."

but I wouldn't say a designer absolutely needs business training. In any case, the job is much more complex today. I'm lucky that Luke is the financial expert. Although I attend every meeting, he has much more experience in this area than I do.

CA: This brings us to the topic of division of labour. Do you make all decisions together? Without compromises?

LM: Luckily, we understand each other so well that we almost always have the same opinion. Some people ask, "How can you even work together?", but I don't know any other way. My parents always worked together too. I think that's a great thing. We don't actually have to make any compromises. When we have a difference of opinion, one ultimately trusts the other. The advantage is that we have the same interests and can therefore always be honest with each other. I see that as an enrichment.

CA: You have been married for 17 years. Was it always your desire to work together?

LM: Yes, we had always talked about it. It happened sooner than we expected. We wanted to do something together. We never specified what exactly or how, but it was our wish.

CA: Would you say that you complete each other? At first glance, your professional backgrounds couldn't be more different: you worked at Louis Vuitton, Balenciaga and Dior; Luke with Supreme and OAMC.

LM: We certainly differ in terms of experience, but ultimately not as much as some might think. Our approach to design is the same. We create in an autobiographical way. How and where we grew up plays a very important part. Me in the confines of the Swiss mountains, where the world came to me, so to speak. Luke in Canada, the ocean in front of the door, looking towards the USA – completely different to me. He is analytical, very curious, always observing what's happening outside. I'm more intuitive and introspective. I think that we complement each other very well.

CA: Would your work look different without this teamwork with your husband?

LM: Probably, yes, but it's difficult for me to imagine how different it would look because we do everything together, and the decisions are always made in agreement. It would certainly be an interesting experiment, but I'm quite happy with our creative process.

CA: In difficult times like these, fashion has to be extravagant and wallow in opulence – at least that's what people used to say. But what we are currently seeing is something more prudent and

5. Fall/Winter 2022 Collection interpreted by Batia Suter. Photo © Jil Sander

in Kanada, den Ozean vor der Tür, den Blick in die USA gerichtet – ganz anders als ich. Er ist analytisch, sehr neugierig, beobachtet immer, was draussen passiert. Ich bin eher intuitiv und introspektiv. Das ergänzt sich sehr gut, finde ich.

CA: Würde denn Deine Arbeit anders aussehen ohne das Teamwork mit Deinem Mann?

LM: Vermutlich schon. Doch wie anders es aussehen würde, das kann ich fiktiv schwer beurteilen, weil wir eben alles zusammen machen und die Entscheidungen immer im Einverständnis erfolgen. Es wäre sicherlich ein interessantes Experiment, aber ich bin mit unserem kreativen Prozess ganz zufrieden.

CA: In schwierigen Zeiten, wie wir sie gerade wieder erleben, muss sich Mode verschwenden, in Opulenz schwelgen – sagte man früher. Doch was wir gerade aktuell sehen, ist eher das Besonnene, das Klassische, ein Comeback der Krawatte. Siehst Du das als Ausdruck eines Bedürfnisses nach Sicherheit. Was fühlt sich für Dich richtig an?

LM: Wir alle haben die Schränke voll mit Kleidern. Es ist nicht so, dass jetzt jemand unbedingt einen neuen Mantel bräuchte. Aber mit dem Klassischen fühlt man sich immer auf der sichereren Seite, es gibt einem Stabilität. Man braucht jedoch auch etwas, was einen neu berührt und bewegt. Das lässt sich schwer generalisieren. Die einen möchten in Opulenz schwelgen, weil ihnen das Sicherheit gibt, die anderen suchen die Stabilität im Klassischen. Ich glaube, Mode funktioniert heute nicht mehr so in Schubladendenken, wie es früher üblich war. Ich persönlich bevorzuge Einfachheit.

CA: Braucht Klarheit im Design Opulenz als Gegensatz, so wie das Schöne erst durch das Hässliche zum Schönen wird?

LM: Ja, durchaus. Es geht doch immer um die Spannung, die durch Gegensätze entsteht. Eine Art unkontrollierbaren Raum, wo diese aufeinandertreffen und man nicht weiss, was passiert.

CA: Sind Modernität und Zeitgeist ein Widerspruch oder macht Modernität den Zeitgeist? Ist Modernität möglicherweise zeitlos?

LM: Wirklich zeitlos gibt es meiner Meinung nach nicht. Ich denke, es steht alles im Kontext mit dem Jetzt. Sogar ein weisses Hemd, vom dem man vielleicht sagen würde, es ist zeitlos. Ist es überhaupt nicht. Man würde nach ein paar Jahren das Volumen nicht mehr als zeitgemäss empfinden, der Kragen ist auf einmal zu klein oder zu gross, die Proportionen generell. Modernität ist das, was sich für mich heute richtig anfühlt. Das ist natürlich auch sehr subjektiv.

6. Kyoto Kiosk Project documented by Nikki McClarron, May 2023. Photo © Nikki McClarron

CA: Damit ist aber auch die Idee, weniger zu konsumieren, weil wir alles schon haben, in Frage zu stellen, oder?

LM: Ich finde, man kann schon weniger konsumieren, dafür aber besser. Es kommt auf die Qualität an. Das perfekte Hemd von damals kann morgen wieder zum perfekten Hemd werden. Wenn ich sage, dass es Zeitlosigkeit nicht gibt, bedeutet dies nicht, dass etwas, das ich vor zehn Jahren kreiert habe und das damals Relevanz hatte, diese nicht auch wieder erlangen kann. Aber die Qualität spielt hier eine wichtige Rolle.

CA: Denkst Du, dass Mode heute noch vorangeht oder eher reagiert?

LM: Ich glaube, es ist beides. Mode ist auf der einen Seite die Reflexion unserer Zeit, aber ich finde auch, dass man mit Mode vorangehen kann. Sie ist ein nonverbales Kommunikationsmittel, das – ganz bewusst, aber auch unbewusst – Botschaften vermittelt: Wie sehe ich mich, wie möchte

«Modernität ist das, was sich für mich heute richtig anfühlt.»

ich gesehen werden? Ich habe einen Freund, der in der Musikbranche arbeitet und auch oft auf der Bühne steht. Er sagt, dass er je nachdem, wie er sich kleidet, anders aufgenommen und wahrgenommen wird.

CA: Gibt es denn das perfekte Design? Wenn ja, was wäre ein Beispiel dafür?

LM: Die Natur.

CA: Du hast an vielen unterschiedlichen Plätzen gelebt und gearbeitet. Hast Du so etwas wie ein Zuhause – eine Heimat?

LM: Ich würde sagen, dass Zermatt meine Heimat ist. Luke hat das gleiche Gefühl gegenüber Vancouver. Aber seitdem wir eine Tochter haben und eine eigene Familie sind, haben wir noch nicht das perfekte neue Zuhause gefunden. Ich sehe uns nicht als Mailänder, obwohl die Stadt so viel bietet und uns soviel gegeben hat. Wie bei allem gilt: Sobald das richtige Gefühl auftritt, werden wir es wissen.

CA: Hat sich denn Deine Arbeit oder auch Dein Design verändert, seitdem Du eine Tochter hast?

LM: Bevor ich Mutter wurde, haben wir gewissermassen im Atelier gelebt, jetzt sind wir viel strikter mit unserer Zeit. Ob sich das Design verändert hat, ist schwierig zu sagen. Bewusst nicht, aber vielleicht unbewusst. Ich machte immer schon am liebsten Sachen, die nicht kompliziert sind, nicht unbequem, die etwas Praktisches, Funktionales haben. Ich mag es pragmatisch. Von daher habe ich auch vor dem Muttersein schon Design bevorzugt, in dem man sich auf jeden Fall wohlfühlt. Vielleicht würde man das jetzt mehr sehen, wenn ich alleine designen würde, doch zusammen mit Luke ist es eben unsere gemeinsame Sprache, die dabei zum Ausdruck kommt.

classic, with even ties staging a comeback. Do you see this as an expression of a need for security? What feels right to you?

LM: We all have closets full of clothes. It's not like anyone really needs a new coat right now. That said, you always feel safe with the classics, they give you stability. However, you also need something that touches and moves you in a new way. This is difficult to generalise. Some want to indulge in opulence because it gives them security, others look for stability in the classics. I think fashion today no longer works in the pigeonholed way it used to. Personally, I prefer simplicity.

CA: Does clarity in design need opulence as a contrast, just as the beautiful only becomes beautiful through the ugly?

LM: Yes, absolutely. It's always about the tension that arises from opposites, a kind of uncontrollable space where they meet, and you don't know what's going to happen.

CA: Are modernity and zeitgeist a contradiction, or does modernity create the zeitgeist? Is modernity perhaps timeless?

LM: In my opinion, there is no such thing as truly timeless. I think everything exists in the context of the now. Even a white shirt, which you might say is timeless, really isn't at all. After a few years you would no longer perceive the volume as contemporary, the collar would suddenly be too

"Modernity is what feels right to me today."

small or too big, and the proportions in general wouldn't be right. Modernity is what feels right to me today. This is of course also very subjective.

CA: This also calls into question the idea of consuming less because we already have everything, right?

LM: I think you can consume less, but better. It all comes down to quality. The perfect shirt from way back when can become the perfect shirt again tomorrow. When I say timelessness doesn't exist, it doesn't mean that something I created ten years ago, which had relevance at the time, can't regain that relevance, but quality plays an important role here.

CA: Do you think fashion today is still moving forward, or is it more reactive?

LM: I think it's both. On the one hand, fashion is a reflection of our times, but I also think that you can move forward with fashion. It is a non-verbal means of communication that conveys messages – both consciously and unconsciously: how do I see myself, how do I want to be seen? I have a friend who works in the music industry and is often on stage. He says that how he dresses affects how he is received and perceived.

CA: Is there such a thing as perfect design? If so, could you give an example?

LM: Nature.

CA: You have lived and worked in many different places. Is there a place you can call home?

LM: I would say that Zermatt is my home. Luke has the same feeling about Vancouver. But since we had a daughter and became a family of our own, we haven't found the perfect new home yet. I don't see us as Milanese, even though the city offers so much and has given us so much. As with anything, we'll know as soon as we get the right feeling.

CA: Has your work or design changed since you had a daughter?

LM: Before I became a mother, we more or less lived in the studio, but now we're much stricter with our time. It's difficult to say whether the design has changed. Not consciously, but perhaps unconsciously. I've always preferred doing things that aren't complicated, aren't uncomfortable, and have something practical and functional about them. I like it pragmatic. That's why, even before becoming a mother, I preferred design that made you feel comfortable. Maybe this would be seen more now if I were designing alone, but together with Luke it's our shared language that's expressed.

7. Resort 2020 Shoes Collection, London, UK, November 2019.
Photo © Chris Rhodes

CA: What does your husband admire you for? What do you admire him for?

LM: He always says I'm so pure. If I like something, it doesn't matter where it comes from, what the reference point is. I don't care. I completely trust my gut feeling. What I admire about him is his knowledge, his insatiable curiosity. If something interests him, he can pursue it and research it for weeks. It's never enough for him. I don't have that patience, but that's why I have him.

CA: You both grew up in monumental nature – you in the Swiss Alps, Luke in British Columbia. What meaning does nature have for you today?

LM: It's incredibly important to us. It's where we feel really good, and we constantly miss it. But nature is also extremely important for our work as a paragon of perfect design that has already solved all problems. "Mother Nature versus Human Nature" is a very important theme for us and was also the starting point and tagline for the issue of *A Magazine* we curated together in 2020. I don't consider myself a city person at all, even though I live and work in a city. With Luke it's more nuanced because he grew up in a real city, Vancouver, surrounded by wild nature on the Pacific Ocean.

CA: Wofür bewundert Dich Dein Mann? Wofür Du ihn?

LM: Er sagt immer, dass ich so pur bin. Wenn mir etwas gefällt, dann ist es egal, woher es kommt, was der Referenzpunkt ist. Das ist für mich nicht wichtig. Ich vertraue da vollkommen meinem Bauchgefühl. Was ich an ihm bewundere, ist sein Wissen, seine unstillbare Neugier. Wenn ihn etwas interessiert, dann kann er dem wochenlang nachgehen und es erforschen. Es ist nie genug für ihn. Ich habe diese Geduld nicht. Aber dafür habe ich ja ihn.

CA: Ihr seid beide in monumentaler Natur – Du in den Schweizer Alpen, Luke in British Columbia – aufgewachsen. Welche Bedeutung hat Natur heute für Dich?

LM: Sie ist unglaublich wichtig für uns. Sie ist der Ort, wo wir uns richtig gut fühlen. Was wir auch konstant vermissen. Die Natur ist aber auch für unsere Arbeit enorm wichtig. Als Vorbild für perfektes Design, das alle Probleme schon gelöst hat. Das Thema «Mother Nature versus Human Nature» beschäftigt uns sehr und war auch der Ausgangspunkt und das Heftmotto für *A Magazine*, das wir 2020 gemeinsam kuratiert haben. Ich empfinde mich überhaupt nicht als Stadtmensch, auch wenn ich dort lebe und arbeite. Bei Luke ist das differenzierter, weil er mit Vancouver in einer richtigen Stadt inmitten wilder Natur am Pazifischen Ozean aufgewachsen ist.

CA: Wenn man sich ganz viel mit Natur und natürlichen Materialien beschäftigt, ist gerade die Ausbeutung der Natur im Zusammenhang mit Mode ein immer wichtigeres Thema. Wie gehst Du damit um?

LM: Das ist ein sehr komplexes Thema. Ich möchte die Natur in meiner Arbeit respektieren und die richtigen Prozesse anwenden, doch das Problem ist die Transparenz, die man einfach nicht hat. Wenn man beispielsweise nur *organic Cotton* verwenden möchte, weiss man gar nicht, ob das nicht vielleicht das grössere Problem schafft. Woher kommt sie? Ist es wirklich *organic Cotton*? Wie viel davon lässt sich überhaupt wirklich nachhaltig produzieren, um die Nachfrage zu befriedigen. Wir hätten zum Beispiel beinahe recyceltes Polyester benutzt, über das wir schlussendlich herausgefunden haben, dass die Plastikflaschen für das Garn extra dafür hergestellt wurden. Das kann natürlich nicht Sinn der Sache sein. Ich glaube, der beste Weg ist es, nur mit Leuten zusammenzuarbeiten, die man kennt und denen man vertraut. Was wir zum Beispiel gleich ganz am Anfang gemacht haben, war das *Packaging* zu analysieren und neu zu kreieren mit recyceltem Papier und Kleiderhängern aus recyceltem Plastik. Oder auch die ganzen Plastikhüllen für die Kleider, die verwendet wurden, bevor diese überhaupt in die Geschäfte kamen. Das haben wir durch Biotech-Materialien ersetzt. Wir versuchen die richtigen Entscheidungen zu treffen, wo wir können.

8. ARC'TERYX × JIL SANDER+ Collaboration, Fall/Winter 2021. Video still © Stephen Kidd

CA: Beeinflussen diese Überlegungen auch den Design-Prozess an sich? Schränkt es ein oder macht es freier?

LM: Es macht freier. Wir verwenden zum Beispiel keine Pelze. Das fühlt sich auch besser an, weil man nicht das Gefühl hat die Natur auszubeuten. Aber ich bin mir natürlich bewusst, dass Mode nicht wirklich der Natur hilft. *Sustainable Fashion* ist am Ende eine Illusion. Es sei denn, man kreiert nur vor Ort mit den Materialien, die man vor Ort findet, und schickt es nirgendwo hin.

CA: Bist Du dennoch radikaler geworden?

LM: Ich würde sagen, ja. Wir schauen viel genauer hin, was nachhaltig ist, und fragen jedes Mal nach, ob es für einen Stoff, den wir ausgesucht haben, eine nachhaltige Version gibt. Wir versuchen, wo wir können, die Fabrikanten und Lieferanten zu animieren, *sustainable* zu agieren. Ich glaube auch, weil immer mehr Designer danach fragen, gibt es mehr Optionen. Das hat schon einen positiven Effekt, selbst wenn die Transparenz nach wie vor ein Problem bleibt. Leider. Ich denke

> «*Sustainable Fashion* ist am Ende eine Illusion. Es sei denn, man kreiert nur vor Ort mit den Materialien, die man vor Ort findet, und schickt es nirgendwo hin.»

auch, dass Nachhaltigkeit kein Marketing-Instrument sein darf, wie es oft passiert. Und Luxus, so wie wir ihn sehen, sollte eigentlich dafür stehen, dass er nachhaltig ist. Das sollte man heute schon voraussetzen können.

CA: Gäbe es ein Label Lucie Meier oder Lucie und Luke Meier, würde dies einen wesentlichen Unterschied machen zu Deiner Arbeit bei Jil Sander?

LM: Ich glaube, ästhetisch wäre es ziemlich gleich, weil unser Designprozess wirklich sehr persönlich ist. Vielleicht wäre es nicht nur Mode, sondern auch andere Designobjekte.

CA: Gibt es eigentlich so etwas wie Freundschaften in der Mode, im Designbereich, in Deiner Branche?

LM: Ich gehe mit dem Wort Freundschaft eher sparsam um. Aber ich habe und hatte das Glück, mit sehr tollen Menschen zu arbeiten, und viele sind Freunde geworden. Das sind vielleicht nicht Namen oder Positionen, die jeder kennen würde. Die Modebranche hat vielleicht nicht einen allzu freundlichen Ruf, doch ich kann sagen, dass ich eigentlich nur gute Erfahrungen gemacht habe und viele, die ich auf meinem Weg kennengelernt habe, mir sehr nahestehen.

CA: Im Modebusiness sind Kooperationen von unterschiedlichen Labels oder Designern heute eigentlich gang und gäbe. Du bist dabei allerdings sehr wählerisch. Die Zusammenarbeit mit

CA: If you deal a lot with nature and natural materials, the exploitation of nature in connection with fashion is an increasingly important topic. How do you deal with it?

LM: This is a very complex topic. I want to respect nature in my work and use the right processes, but the problem is transparency, it just isn't there. For example, if you only want to use organic cotton, you don't know whether that might create a bigger problem. Where does it come from? Is it really organic? How much of it can actually be produced organically to meet demand? For example, we almost used recycled polyester, but we eventually found out that the plastic bottles were made specifically for the yarn. That obviously doesn't make sense. I think the best way is to work only with people you know and trust. One thing we did right at the beginning was to analyse the packaging and switch to using recycled paper and clothes hangers made from recycled plastic. Then there were all the plastic covers used to protect the clothes before they even hit the stores. We replaced them with biotech materials. We try to make the right decisions where we can.

CA: Do these considerations also influence the design process itself? Do they restrict you or free you up?

LM: They make you freer. For example, we don't use fur. The clothes feel better because you don't have the feeling that you're exploiting nature. I am aware, of course, that fashion doesn't really help nature. In the end, sustainable fashion is an illusion – unless you only create it locally with locally sourced materials and don't send it anywhere.

CA: Have you nevertheless become more radical?

LM: I would say so, yes. We take a much closer look at what is sustainable and always ask whether there's a sustainable version of a material we've chosen. Wherever we can, we try to encourage manufacturers and suppliers to act sustainably. I also think that, because more and more designers are asking for it, there are more options. That does have a positive effect, even if transparency sadly remains a problem. I also think that sustainability should not be a marketing tool, as is often the case. Luxury, as we see it, should actually mean sustainable too. You should be able to assume that today.

9. Fall/Winter 2021
JIL SANDER+ COLLECTION.
Photo © Nikki McClarron

"In the end, *sustainable* fashion is an illusion – unless you only create it locally with locally sourced materials and don't send it anywhere."

CA: If there were a Lucie Meier or Lucie and Luke Meier label, would it be significantly different compared with your work at Jil Sander?

LM: I think, aesthetically, it would be pretty much the same because our design process is really very personal. Maybe it wouldn't just be fashion, but also other design objects.

CA: Is there actually such a thing as friendships in fashion, in design, in your industry?

LM: I use the word "friendship" rather sparingly, but I have been lucky enough over the years to work with some very great people, and many of them have become friends. They're perhaps not all household names. The fashion industry may not have a reputation for being all that friendly, but I can say that I've only had good experiences, and many of those I've met along the way are very close to me.

CA: In the fashion business, collaborations between different labels or designers are now common practice. However, you are very selective. Collaborations with companies like Birkenstock or Arc'Teryx are the exception. Where does this reluctance come from?

LM: When we created the Jil Sander+ line in 2019, we wanted to expand the main collection with a range of models intended for life outside the city, very utilitarian clothes for trips to the countryside, the sea, the mountains. Jil Sander for nature, so to speak. To reinforce the concept, we wanted to work with companies that have the techniques we don't have, so it's a question of cooperating to create something new that neither we nor the partner company could create alone. This is how the cooperations with Birkenstock and Arc'Teryx came about – two names that have always been in our lives. I grew up with Birkenstocks, Luke with Arc'Teryx from and in Vancouver. It was important for us to create these lines because nature is so important to us, and we enjoy spending time in it.

CA: If you had to describe your work in one sentence, what would it be?

LM: My work might not save lives, but I hope that I can give people something good and try to improve people's everyday lives or make them easier if I can boost their self-confidence in some way with our clothes.

CA: What does it mean to you to be awarded the highest honour in your homeland, the Swiss Grand Award for Design?

LM: I really feel very honoured. It's also important to me because I've always felt Swiss, but until

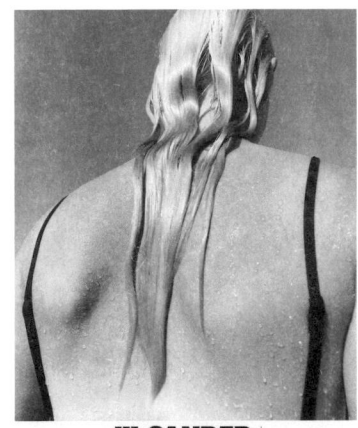

10. Spring/Summer 2022
JIL SANDER+ COLLECTION
Photo © Nikki McClarron

Firmen wie Birkenstock oder Arc'Teryx sind die Ausnahme. Woher kommt diese Zurückhaltung?

LM: Als wir 2019 die Linie Jil Sander+ kreiert haben, wollten wir die Hauptkollektion um eine Reihe von Modellen erweitern, die für das Leben ausserhalb der Stadt gedacht sind. Sehr utilitaristisch für Reisen aufs Land, ans Meer, in die Berge. Jil Sander für die Natur gewissermassen.

«Auch wenn ich keine Leben rette mit meiner Arbeit, hoffe ich doch, dass ich den Leuten etwas Gutes geben kann [...].»

Um das Konzept zu verstärken, wollten wir mit Firmen zusammenarbeiten, die über die Techniken verfügen, die wir nicht haben. Also eine Kooperation, um etwas Neues zu schaffen, das wir alleine nicht kreieren können und die Partnerfirma auch nicht alleine. So kam es zu der Kooperation mit Birkenstock und Arc'Teryx. Zwei Namen, die schon immer in unserem Leben waren. Ich bin mit Birkenstocks aufgewachsen, Luke mit Arc'Teryx aus und in Vancouver. Für uns war es wichtig, diese Linien zu kreieren, weil uns eben die Natur so wichtig ist und wir uns selbst so gerne in ihr aufhalten.

CA: Wenn Du Deine Arbeit in einem Satz charakterisieren müsstest, wie würde dieser lauten?

LM: Auch wenn ich keine Leben rette mit meiner Arbeit, hoffe ich doch, dass ich den Leuten etwas Gutes geben kann, und versuche, Menschen den Alltag zu verbessern oder zu erleichtern, wenn ich mit unseren Kleidern zu ihrem Selbstvertrauen etwas beitragen kann.

CA: Was bedeutet es für Dich, mit dem höchsten Designpreis deiner Heimat, dem Schweizer Grand Prix Design, ausgezeichnet zu werden?

LM: Ich fühle mich wirklich sehr geehrt. Es ist auch deshalb wichtig für mich, weil ich mich immer als Schweizerin gefühlt habe, es aber bis vor sieben Jahren auf dem Papier nicht war. Ich bin zwar hier geboren, aufgewachsen und zur Schule gegangen. Doch die Schweizer Nationalität erhielt ich offiziell erst durch meine Heirat mit Luke, weil meine Mutter Österreicherin ist und mein Vater aus Deutschland stammt.

CA: Empfindest Du diese Auszeichnung als Zwischenstation oder als Höhepunkt deines kreativen Schaffens?

LM: Ich habe überhaupt nicht damit gerechnet und umso mehr freut es mich. Ich betrachte dies als Anerkennung meines bisherigen Tuns. Mode ist ein sehr abstraktes Gebiet. Viele Menschen haben gar keine Vorstellung davon, wie selbstverzehrend die Arbeit darin ist, wie sie dein Leben bestimmt. Was den Höhepunkt meines kreativen Schaffens betrifft, hoffe ich doch sehr, dass mir in Zukunft noch einiges mehr gelingen wird.

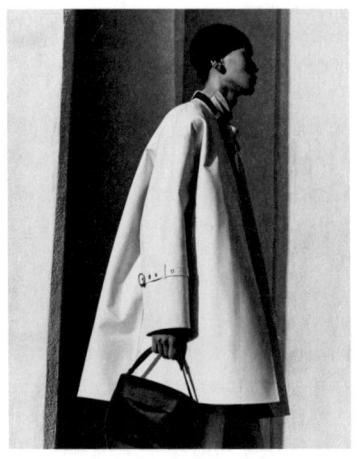

11. Spring/Summer 2024 Collection documented by Jack Davison.
Photo © Jack Davison

Christiane Arp war von 2003 bis 2020 Chefredakteurin der deutschen VOGUE. Die studierte Modedesignerin ist Gründungsmitglied und Vorstandsvorsitzende des Fashion Council Germany. Sie gilt als eine der wichtigsten Nachwuchsförderinnen junger Designtalente und kennt Lucie Meier und ihren Mann seit vielen Jahren.

Das Gespräch wurde moderiert und aufgezeichnet von Robert Emich. Emich war von 2006 bis 2020 stellvertretender Chefredakteur der deutschen VOGUE und ist heute Chefredakteur des Health- und Lifestylemagazins Premium Quarterly.

seven years ago I wasn't on paper. I was born, grew up and went to school here, but I only officially received Swiss nationality when I married Luke. That's because my mother is Austrian and my father comes from Germany.

CA: Do you see this award as a milestone or a highlight of your creative career?

LM: I didn't expect it at all, which makes me all the happier about it. I see this as recognition of what I've achieved so far. Fashion is a very abstract field. Many people have no idea how all-consuming the work is and how it takes over your life. As far as the pinnacle of my creative career is concerned, I really hope that I still have a lot to achieve in the future.

Christiane Arp was Editor-in-Chief of German VOGUE from 2003 to 2020. She has a degree in fashion design and is a founding member and chairwoman of the Fashion Council Germany. She is regarded as one of the most important promoters of young design talent and has known Lucie Meier and her husband for many years.

The interview was moderated and recorded by Robert Emich. Emich was Deputy Editor-in-Chief of German VOGUE from 2006 to 2020 and is now Editor-in-Chief of the health and lifestyle magazine Premium Quarterly.

G

J, K

Lucie Meier   Per istinto

di Christiane Arp

Se Lucie Meier volesse esprimere il proprio genio creativo in modo diverso rispetto al fashion design non lo farebbe attraverso le parole, afferma. Gliene bastano poche per svelarci il suo intimo. Una sola per lei è sufficiente quando le viene chiesto di darci un esempio di design perfetto: «natura».

Questa risposta ci fornisce immediatamente una visione del suo universo creativo. Non si tratta di una trasfigurazione romantica, ma piuttosto di una sorta di dialogo intuitivo alla ricerca di una soluzione creativa, materiale e «naturale», ispirato all'origine da un'opera d'arte, un libro, o forse anche da un sentimento o da un particolare momento della vita. Da sette anni Lucie Meier porta avanti questo processo creativo in collaborazione con suo marito Luke per il marchio Jil Sander, stabilendo nuovi standard (etici ed estetici) nell'industria della moda. «Evoluzione in corso», così la descrive. Per Lucie Meier il processo creativo è in continuo mutamento, cercare la novità a tutti i costi non rispecchia la sua filosofia: «Tutto ciò che creiamo deve avere un senso, deve toccarci da vicino».

La sensazione tattile ed emotiva che procurano gli abiti la affascina fin da piccola. Lucie Mennig, cresciuta a Zermatt, ai piedi del Cervino, dove la sua famiglia – prima i suoi genitori e ora il fratello con la moglie – gestisce il ristorante «Zum See» in uno chalet di oltre 500 anni, sa bene fin da subito che il suo futuro sarà nella moda. Una passione nata dall'amore della madre per i tessuti, la moda, e in particolare il brand Jil Sander.

È così che Lucie Meier decide di scoprire questo nuovo mondo trasferendosi a Firenze per studiare fashion marketing al Polimoda. Si tratta però di una breve parentesi, in quanto presto capisce che quell'ambito della moda non è ciò che desidera. Tuttavia il periodo trascorso all'università italiana segna il corso della sua vita: qui incontra Luke Meier, un giovane canadese con radici svizzere che qualche anno più tardi diventerà suo marito. Insieme si trasferiscono a New York, dove Lucie inizia a lavorare per la rivista Nylon. Poi decide di studiare fashion design ed entra all'École de la Chambre Syndicale di Parigi. A conclusione del percorso di studi svolge uno stage presso Louis Vuitton sotto la guida di Marc Jacobs. «Un'esperienza incredibile», come lei stessa afferma, cui seguono cinque anni di lavoro nel team del geniale visionario della moda. La tappa successiva non è meno importante: da Balenciaga crea le collezioni di sfilata del leggendario brand assieme a Nicolas Ghesquière. Si tratta di due geni creativi completamente diversi: «Per Marc Jacobs si creava una collezione in tre settimane, con Nicolas Ghesquière ci prendevamo sei mesi di tempo». Trova infine la strada per Dior, dove Lucie Meier diventa head designer per la collezione estiva sotto la direzione creativa di Raf Simons. Quando alla fine del 2015 Simons lascia la maison francese, Lucie Meier ne assume la gestione ad interim insieme a Serge Ruffieux, fino all'arrivo di Maria Grazia Chiuri nel 2016.

Il sogno di arrivare alla direzione creativa di Jil Sander si avvera «prima del previsto» nel 2017: non solo inizia a lavorare per il suo brand preferito sin dall'infanzia, ma per giunta lo fa assieme al marito. Per quanto diverso possa essere il loro background professionale, la coppia si bilancia alla perfezione: da una parte Lucie, che crea d'istinto e con profonda intuizione, dall'altra Luke, che con passione e spirito analitico esamina i processi. In questa collaborazione lui ammira «la sua calma, la sua intuizione e la sua infallibile memoria fotografica». Insieme cercano nuovi percorsi per conferire alla moda senso e bellezza, in tempi in cui il rigido pensiero classificatorio tra opulenza e minimalismo è spinto fino all'assurdo. Cercano il loro linguaggio attraverso la tensione creata dagli opposti, per alimentare il fuoco dell'essenza creativa.

Nel compiacente mondo della moda che cerca di attirare l'attenzione a tutti i costi Lucie Meier rappresenta un'eccezione degna di nota: viene vista e ascoltata proprio perché, con grande imperturbabilità di spirito, ha trovato un percorso creativo sostenibile che molti stanno ancora affannosamente cercando.

I suoi lavori si contraddistinguono per l'introduzione di nuovi materiali, l'implementazione e la verificabilità di processi sostenibili, ma anche le linee contemporanee con una qualità senza tempo. «Tutti noi abbiamo gli armadi pieni di vestiti», afferma Lucie Meier, «Nessuno di noi ha necessariamente bisogno di un nuovo cappotto. Piuttosto abbiamo bisogno di qualcosa che ci tocchi da vicino e ci emozioni. Spero di riuscire a dare alle persone qualcosa di bello e cerco di migliorare la loro vita quotidiana contribuendo con i miei capi a renderla più semplice e ad aumentare in qualche modo la loro fiducia in sé stessi».

Christiane Arp è stata caporedattrice di VOGUE Germania dal 2003 al 2020. Laureata in fashion design, è membro fondatore e presidente del comitato direttivo del Fashion Council Germany. È considerata una delle più importanti promotrici di giovani talenti del design e conosce Lucie Meier e suo marito da molti anni.

Lucie Meier   By instinct

by Christiane Arp

If Lucie Meier wanted another way to express herself creatively apart from fashion design, she says, she would not choose words. Just a few words are all she needs to reveal her inner self. When asked to give an example of perfect design, she only needs one: "nature". This response instantly provides an insight into her creative cosmos. It is not a romantic transfiguration but an intuitive dialogue that strives for a material, creative, natural solution – originally taking inspiration from a work of art, a book, perhaps even a feeling, "a moment in my life". For seven years now, she has brought this creative process to bear in partnership with her husband Luke at Jil Sander, setting new standards (both aesthetic and ethical) in the fashion industry. "Evolution in progress" is how she describes it. She cannot bear the thought of creating something new just for the sake of newness: "Everything we create must have a meaning, must touch us."

The tactile and emotional feeling of clothing fascinated her from an early age. Growing up as Lucie Mennig at the foot of the Matterhorn in Zermatt, where her family – first her parents, now her brother and his wife – still runs the restaurant Zum See in a chalet that is more than 500 years old, Lucie Meier already knew very early on that she wanted to work in fashion one way or another. She caught the bug from her mother, who loves fabrics and fashion – especially Jil Sander.

Her first steps into the fashion world took her to Polimoda in Florence, where she began to study fashion marketing. This turned out to be a brief stint as it quickly became clear to her that this area of fashion was not really where she wanted to be. Nevertheless, her time at the Italian university set the course for her later life because it was here that she met and fell in love with a young Canadian with Swiss roots named Luke Meier. They moved to New York together, and Lucie started working for *Nylon* magazine. She decided to study fashion design and applied to the École de la Chambre Syndicale in Paris. She then joined Louis Vuitton as an intern under Marc Jacobs. "An incredible experience," she says, which turned into a five-year commitment as a designer in the brilliant fashion visionary's team. Her next stop was no less high-profile: at Balenciaga, she created the legendary label's show collection with Nicolas Ghesquière. A rollercoaster of creative genius: "With Marc Jacobs, we created an entire collection in three weeks, whereas Nicolas Ghesquière and I took six months." She ultimately found her way to Dior, becoming head designer of the summer team under Raf Simons. After his departure at the end of 2015, she ran the couture house with Serge Ruffieux on an interim basis until Maria Grazia Chiuri took over in 2016.

The call to become creative director of Jil Sander in 2017 was a wish fulfilled – "sooner than expected": not only was it her favourite label from childhood, it was also an opportunity to work with her husband. The professional backgrounds of the two could not be more different, but they gelled together as a team very quickly. Lucie creates intuitively straight from her gut, while Luke passionately analyses and researches processes. When working together, he admires "her calmness, her intuition and her absolutely infallible photographic memory". Together they look for ways to bring meaning and beauty to fashion in an age that seems to push the conventional dichotomy of opulence versus minimalism to ever more absurd extremes, for a way to harness the tension arising from opposites, for a kind of creative essence.

In the complacent fashion world that seeks to attract attention at all costs, Lucie Meier is an exception who is seen and heard precisely because she has calmly found the sort of sustainable creative path that so many others are still frantically searching for.

A lot of it is about new materials, knowing how to use them and finding verifiably sustainable processes, but it is also about contemporary lines with a timeless quality. "We all have closets full of clothes," says Lucie Meier. "It's not like anyone necessarily needs a new coat, but you do need something that touches and moves you. I hope that I can give people something good and try to improve people's everyday lives or make them easier if I can boost their self-confidence in some way."

Christiane Arp was Editor-in-Chief of German VOGUE from 2003 to 2020. She has a degree in fashion design and is a founding member and chairwoman of the Fashion Council Germany. She is regarded as one of the most important promoters of young design talent and has known Lucie Meier and her husband for many years.

[DE → p. 9, FR → p. 10]

Biography

Born in Zermatt (Visp) in 1982
Daughter to a German father and an Austrian mother. Raised in Zermatt.

1996–2001 Studied at the Kollegium Brig and graduated at the Collège de Saint Maurice, with a focus on language studies.

2001–03 Moved to Florence to study Fashion Marketing at Polimoda, where she also met her future husband Luke Meier.

2003 Moved to New York City and interned at *Nylon* magazine.

2004–07 Moved to Paris to study Fashion Design and Patternmaking at the École de la Chambre Syndicale de la Couture Parisienne.

2005 Internship at Narciso Rodriguez in New York City, working mainly in the atelier on patterns for the show collection.

2006 Internship at Chloé in Paris, with focus on embroideries, volume and detail research for the show collection.

2007 Final scholastic collection show in Paris. Won the Trophée Saint Roch for most exceptional collection.
Got married to Luke Meier at City Hall in New York City.
Began an internship at Louis Vuitton, joining the small design team working with Marc Jacobs on women's ready to wear shows and pre-collections.

2008 Received a permanent position within the Louis Vuitton women's design studio under the direction of Marc Jacobs. Worked on garment design, draping, and embroideries for show and pre-collections. Worked closely with the in-house ateliers as well as Parisian and foreign embroidery companies. This was the initial experience of playing an integral part in the entire lifecycle of a fashion show.

2012 Joined Balenciaga to work with Nicolas Ghesquière as Senior Designer on the main collections. Worked deeply on shows and managed a small team of designers.

2014 Joined Christian Dior to work with Raf Simons as Head Designer of summer collections. Worked on the haute couture and ready-to-wear collections, managed a large team of designers and worked hand in hand with the ateliers.

2015 Co-Creative Director of Christian Dior. Designed five collections, including ready to wear and haute couture, accessories, print and embroideries. Was jointly responsible for the direction of the music, set design, casting, and hair and makeup of the collections.

2017 Was chosen with her husband Luke Meier to be the Creative Directors of Jil Sander in Milan, with Spring/Summer 2018 being their debut show.

2018 École de la Chambre Syndicale mentorship participant, accompanied students through the creation of their final collections.
Spring/Summer 2018 and Fall/Winter 2018 Campaign project with Wim Wenders.
Jil Sander Tokyo Omotesando store opened as a first project designed in partnership with John Pawson, Kelsey Lu performed during the opening.

2019 Spring/Summer 2019 Campaign project with Mario Sorrenti, a road trip through Japan.
Launch of Jil Sander+, including a collaboration with Mackintosh.
Collaboration with artist Linda Tegg to create the installation *Adjacent Field* during Salone del Mobile in Milan, documented by Larry Fink.
Kelsey Lu performed live at the Fall/Winter 2019 show.
Fall/Winter 2019 Campaign project with Nigel Shafran, a road trip through Scotland.
Together with Luke was elected Leading Professors of the Fashion Department of the Angewandte in Vienna. Created a new curriculum, explored the individuality of the students, and challenged their notions of fashion in today's world.

2020 Spring/Summer 2020 Campaign project with Olivier Kervern.
Jil Sander Publishing, presented for the first time at Jil Sander Via Sant'Andrea space in Milan. *Sicily*, an expansive representation of the campaign, is the first publication.
Guest curator of *A Magazine curated by*.
Fall/Winter 2020 Campaign project with Mario Sorrenti, Chris Rhodes, Anders Edström, Lina Scheynius, Olivier Kervern.

2021	Ella Rose Maria Meier was born. Spring/Summer 2021 Campaign project with Shaniqwa Jarvis, Bibi Borthwick, Drew Jarret and Nigel Shafran. Jil Sander+ collaboration projects with Birkenstock and Arc'teryx. Fall/Winter 2021 Campaign project with Joel Meyerowitz.	Jil Sander Publishing
2022	Spring/Summer 2022 Campaign project with Chris Rhodes in Paris. Pre-Fall 2022 imagery photographed by Chris Rhodes, alongside interpretive collaged and painted works by Katrien De Blauwer. Fall/Winter 2022 Campaign project with Chris Rhodes. Fall/Winter 2022 Collection interpreted by Batia Suter at Standby Gallery Tokyo.	2020 Sicily 2020 Familiarity 2021 Proximity 2021 Tuscany 2022 Macro 2022 Paris 2023 L.A. 2023 Manchester
2023	Spring/Summer 2023 Campaign project with Chris Rhodes in LA. Jil Sander London store opened, as first project designed in partnership with architects Casper Müller Kneer. Fall/Winter 2023 Campaign project with Chris Rhodes featuring Jeff Mills in Manchester.	
2024	Spring/Summer 2024 Campaign project with Jack Davison. Mk.Gee performed live at the Fall/Winter show.	

Gran Premio svizzero di design 2024

Il Gran Premio svizzero di design omaggia carriere esemplari e offre visibilità a designer il cui lavoro apre prospettive o riflessioni particolarmente interessanti in questo campo.

Quali voci far sentire in un mondo così rumoroso come il nostro? Bisogna valorizzare coloro che generano idee per rendere più belli i nostri oggetti, i nostri manifesti, i nostri siti Internet e i nostri vestiti? Oppure coloro che li rendono più sostenibili? O forse va premiato chi vede nel design un atto sociale? Questa disciplina può essere portatrice di nuovi messaggi? Cosa significa, nel 2024, pensare e creare tenendo conto della diversità e della complessità del nostro mondo?

La giuria discute intensamente di questi temi e valuta con la massima attenzione il messaggio che intende trasmettere con l'attribuzione dei tre premi. Il suo intento è sempre quello di mettere in evidenza il lavoro di singoli individui che si distinguono per il loro approccio innovativo, creativo o impegnato oppure hanno influenzato o influenzano ancora in modo significativo la loro disciplina. E questo senza dimenticare le donne, che in passato hanno ricevuto poca visibilità. L'annuncio dei Gran Premi attira l'attenzione dei media e consente di far conoscere i diversi ambiti del design a un pubblico diversificato, ma non solo: il riconoscimento federale, conferito da pari, rende anche omaggio a professionisti e professioniste che esplorano i confini della propria pratica.

Nel 2024 sono state scelte persone che hanno intrapreso un percorso innovativo nel loro campo. Il contributo di Paola De Martin va ben oltre la ricerca tradizionale. Le sue riflessioni critiche guardano al design con un approccio transdisciplinare che si colloca in un determinato contesto sociale e politico e affronta questioni come la migrazione, il razzismo e l'esclusione sociale. La stilista Lucie Meier è protagonista di una carriera straordinaria: a soli 40 anni ha già lavorato per importanti case di moda come Louis Vuitton, Balenciaga, Dior et Jil Sander. Chi costruisce il proprio percorso professionale all'estero deve spesso attendere molto tempo prima che il suo operato venga riconosciuto in Svizzera. Il premio a Lucie Meier valorizza una designer che conosce nel profondo la propria disciplina. Infine, con i suoi 74 anni, Luciano Rigolini è un creatore che non ha mai smesso di interrogare le immagini. Esplora la sua materia facendola propria e si interessa in particolare alla fotografia vernacolare. Attraverso il suo sguardo, le fotografie rivelano nuove potenzialità plastiche. Tutto questo avviene in parallelo a una carriera internazionale comme produttore nel cinema documentario d'autore.

Riunendo sotto l'egida del Gran Premio svizzero di design 2024 tre personalità che si trovano in momenti diversi del loro percorso professionale e perseguono ognuna un approccio del tutto singolare, la giuria mostra che il

design apre molteplici prospettive. Riconoscere il lavoro di Paola De Martin, Lucie Meier e Luciano Rigolini, attivi in ambiti relativamente distanti fra loro, significa proprio questo. Le loro storie personali sono la prova che non è necessario appartenere a un'élite per aspirare al riconoscimento del proprio operato, perché gli elementi propulsori della loro creatività sono la riflessione e l'impegno.

Nathalie Herschdorfer, Presidente della Commissione federale del design

Prefazione

A 18 anni dal lancio, il Gran Premio svizzero di Design dell'Ufficio federale della cultura (UFC), il più alto riconoscimento per il design in Svizzera, continua a essere uno strumento eccezionale per mettere in luce le molteplici espressioni del design e la varietà degli sviluppi professionali in questo campo. Grazie alla valorizzazione di prospettive e approcci diversi, il nostro sguardo sull'importanza del design nella società diventa ogni anno più ricco e dinamico.

La prima edizione del Gran Premio svizzero di design si è tenuta nel 2007. Poco tempo prima l'UFC aveva abbandonato lo strumento dei contributi ai progetti di design e la Commissione federale del design (CFD) era alla ricerca di nuove possibilità per fornire a chi un sostegno finanziario mirato e proattivo alle eccellenze nel design.

Il primo anno, su proposta della CFD, sono stati assegnati cinque premi del valore di 40 000 franchi ciascuno. Due sono andati a personalità di fama internazionale: Adrian Frutiger, importante creatore di caratteri tipografici, e Bernhard Schobinger, uno dei più influenti designer di gioielli in Europa. Gli altri tre, invece, hanno voluto essere un riconoscimento alla generazione emergente e sono stati attribuiti all'agenzia Nose, fondata nel 1991, alla stilista Ruth Grüninger e al grafico Cornel Windlin, allora poco più che quarantenne. L'obiettivo dell'UFC era consentire a designer di talento di dedicarsi a progetti innovativi e sviluppare il loro potenziale creativo senza doversi concentrare esclusivamente sul successo commerciale.

I premi hanno segnato un pezzo di storia del design svizzero. La pubblicazione contiene spesso primi elementi d'archivio che poi serviranno come base per future presentazioni delle creazioni e per la ricerca. Proprio l'anno scorso si sono accesi i riflettore su diversi vincitori e vincitrici delle edizioni precedenti del Gran Premio svizzero di design: il Museo nazionale svizzero ha allestito una mostra monografica sull'eccezionale talento della stilista Ursula Rodel (premiata nel 2009); a settembre è stato pubblicato un catalogo completo dei lavori di Rosmarie Baltensweiler (premiata nel 2019), visionaria designer di lampade; Eleonore Peduzzi Riva (premiata nel 2023), l'architetta e designer che ha contribuito a sviluppare il celebre divano DS 600 e molto altro ancora, è stata più volte intervistata e invitata a partecipare a tavole rotonde; il Museum für Gestaltung di Zurigo ha esposto recentemente i magnifici tessuti di Claudia Caviezel (premiata nel 2016); Sarah Kueng e Lovis Caputo (premiate nel 2020) hanno ricevuto il meritato Goldene Hase della rivista Hochparterre, e la casa editrice About Books sta per pubblicare un volume con 12 nuovi tipi di carattere ideati da Rosmarie Tissi (premiata nel 2018).

Le vincitrici e il vincitore di quest'anno, Paola De Martin, Lucie Meier e Luciano Rigolini, hanno in comune la capacità di mettere in discussione le tradizioni e percorrere nuove strade. Con il loro approccio innovativo contribuiscono a promuovere la diversità, l'inclusione, l'etica, la collaborazione e la tecnologia nella cultura. Scoprite come tra le pagine di questa pubblicazione, che spero possa essere ricca di spunti interessanti e, come ogni anno, fonte di ispirazione per i vostri progetti futuri.

Anna Niederhäuser
Responsabile di design
Ufficio federale della cultura

Swiss Grand Award for Design 2024

The Swiss Grand Award for Design honours outstanding careers and casts a spotlight on creators whose work breaks new ground or explores interesting new intellectual avenues in this domain.

Which voices should we allow to be heard amidst the clamour of our world? Should we favour those whose creativity makes our objects, posters, websites or clothes more beautiful? What about those who make them more sustainable, or those who view design as a social practice? Can design convey new messages? What, in 2024, does it mean to think and create while acknowledging the diversity and complexity of our world?

The Jury engages in vigorous debate on these questions and pays a great deal of attention to the message it wishes to send out with its choice of three winners. It wants to showcase individuals with particularly innovative, creative or activist approaches as well as those that have influenced or continue to influence their discipline in a significant way – without forgetting women, of course, who were less visible in the past especially. The announcement of the Grand Award winners attracts media attention and gives the various design disciplines exposure to a broader public. An award sponsored by the federal government and handed out by peers is also a way of paying tribute to professionals who push the envelope in their chosen field and leave their mark on it through innovation, creativity or activism.

For 2024, we have chosen three innovators. Paola De Martin's work goes way beyond traditional research. She takes a critical view and a transdisciplinary approach to design, embedding it in a sociopolitical context by relating it to issues of migration, racism and social exclusion. The fashion designer Lucie Meier has had an enviable international career to date. Still only 40, she has worked for some of the great fashion houses, including Louis Vuitton, Balenciaga, Dior and Jil Sander. Recognition in Switzerland often comes late to those who pursue a career abroad, but Lucie Meier deserves this award due to her excellent, nuanced mastery of her craft. For his part, 74-year-old Luciano Rigolini has never tired of questioning images. He explores his material through appropriation, taking a particularly keen interest in vernacular photography and unlocking new dimensions of sculpturally. At the same time, he has pursued an international as a producer in auteur documentary films.

In selecting three individuals at different stages in their professional lives for the Swiss Grand Award for Design 2024, each with their own unique approach, the Jury highlights the variety of perspectives design can open up. The practices of Paola De Martin, Lucie Meier and Luciano Rigolini have relatively little in common and thus demonstrate the many career paths designers are free to choose. Their personal stories make it clear that

recognition does not hinge on being part of an elite: it can come through considered, committed creativity.

Nathalie Herschdorfer, Chair of the Federal Design Commission

Introduction

Even 18 years after the Swiss Grand Award for Design was launched, this highest honour for Swiss designers remains an outstanding instrument for the Federal Office of Culture (FOC) to showcase the wide range of potential career paths and the diversity of the design field. As we recognise a variety of different perspectives and approaches, our understanding of the importance of design for society as a whole is enriched and enlivened year by year.

The Grand Award was first presented in 2007. At that time, the FOC had recently discontinued its design project subsidies, and the Federal Design Commission was looking for new, more targeted and proactive ways to support designers with funding.

Five awards worth CHF 40,000 each were handed out in the first year at the Commission's suggestion. The winners included two internationally renowned personalities: the type designer Adrian Frutiger and Bernhard Schobinger, one of Europe's most influential jewellery artists. At the same time, the younger generation was represented by the design agency Nose, founded in 1991, as well as fashion designer Ruth Grüninger and graphic artist Cornel Windlin, who had only just turned 40. The FOC's aim was to enable design practitioners to work on innovative projects and develop their creative potential without having to focus solely on commercial success.

The Grand Award encapsulates a piece of Swiss design history. The accompanying publication often contains previously unseen archive pictures and serves as a basis for future work presentations and research projects. Just last year, a number of former winners were back in the spotlight. The Swiss National Museum hosted a monographic exhibition of the exceptionally talented Swiss fashion designer Ursula Rodel (Grand Award winner in 2009). An extensive catalogue of works by lighting design pioneer Rosmarie Baltensweiler (winner in 2019) was published in September. Eleonore Peduzzi Riva (winner in 2023), who had a hand in far more than just the world-famous DS-600 sofa, was invited to a number of panels and interviews. Zurich's Museum für Gestaltung presented the wonderful textile works of Claudia Caviezel (winner in 2016), while at the end of the year, Sarah Kueng and Lovis Caputo (winners in 2020) received a well-deserved Golden Hare award from *Hochparterre* magazine. We are also delighted to see a brand-new work by Rosmarie Tissi (winner in 2018), comprising 12 new alphabets, published by About Books.

This year's winners – Paola De Martin, Lucie Meier and Luciano Rigolini – are all trailblazers who have succeeded in questioning traditions. Read on to find out how their groundbreaking work has promoted diversity, inclusion, ethics, cooperation and technology in cultural circles. I hope you find their stories fascinating and, like every year, take inspiration from them for your own projects.

Anna Niederhäuser
Head of Design
Federal Office of Culture

[DE → p. 3, FR → p. 5]

Swiss Grand Award for Design Winners 2007–24

2024
Paola De Martin
  Designer and design researcher
Lucie Meier
  Fashion designer and creative director
Luciano Rigolini
  Photographer and producer for auteur documentary films

2023
Etienne Delessert
  Illustrator and graphic designer
Eleonore Peduzzi Riva
  Interior architect and consultant
Chantal Prod'Hom
  Museum director and curator

2022
Susanne Bartsch
  Talent curator and event producer
Verena Huber
  Interior architect
Beat Streuli
  Artist

2021
Julia Born
  Graphic designer
Peter Knapp
  Photographer and art director
Sarah Owens
  Design educator and researcher

2020
Ida Gut
  Fashion designer
Monique Jacot
  Photographer
Kueng Caputo
  Product designers

2019
Rosmarie Baltensweiler
  Product designer
Connie Hüsser
  Interior stylist
Thomi Wolfensberger
  Lithographer and publisher

2018
Cécile Feilchenfeldt
  Textile designer
Felco
  Product design
Rosmarie Tissi
  Graphic designer

2017
David Bielander
  Jewellery designer
Thomas Ott
  Illustrator
Jean Widmer
  Graphic designer and art director

2016
Claudia Caviezel
  Textile designer
Hans Eichenberger
  Product and interior designer
Ralph Schraivogel
  Graphic designer

2015
Luc Chessex
  Photographer
Lora Lamm
  Graphic designer
Team '77
  Typographers and type designers

2014
Erich Biehle
  Textile designer
Alfredo Häberli
  Furniture and product designer
Wolfgang Weingart
  Typographer

2013
Trix & Robert Haussmann
  Interior and product designers
Armin Hofmann
  Graphic designer
Martin Leuthold
  Textile designer

2012
Franco Clivio
  Product designer
Gavillet & Rust
  Graphic designers
Karl Gerstner
  Graphic designer

2011
Jörg Boner
  Product designer
NORM
  Graphic designers
Ernst Scheidegger
  Photographer
Walter Steiger
  Footwear designer

2010
Susi & Ueli Berger
  Furniture designers
Jean-Luc Godard
  Filmmaker
Sonnhild Kestler
  Textile designer
Otto Künzli
  Jewellery designer

2009
Robert Frank
  Photographer
Christoph Hefti
  Textile designer
Ursula Rodel
  Fashion designer
Thut Möbel
  Furniture design

2008
Holzer Kobler Architekturen
  Exhibition designers and architects
Albert Kriemler (Akris)
  Fashion designer
Alain Kupper
  Graphic designer, musician and artist
Walter Pfeiffer
  Photographer

2007
Ruth Grüninger
  Fashion designer
NOSE
  Communication design, service design
Bernhard Schobinger
  Jewellery designer
Adrian Frutiger
  Type desinger
Cornel Windlin
  Graphic designer

Swiss Federal Design Commission 2024

Chair
Nathalie Herschdorfer
  Director, Photo Élysée

Members
Cécile Feilchenfeldt
  Textile designer, Paris
Davide Fornari
  Professor for Research and Development at ECAL, Renens
David Glättli
  Industrial designer and creative director, Zurich/ Tokyo
Andreas Gysin
  Programmer and graphic designer, Lugano
Vera Sacchetti
  Design critic and curator, Basel
Ivan Sterzinger
  Graphic designer and publisher, Zurich

Colophon

Published on the occasion of the Swiss Grand Award for Design 2024

Head of project
  Anna Niederhäuser
  Federal Office of Culture (FOC), Bern

Editing, project coordination
  Mirjam Fischer
  mille pages, Zurich

Art direction and design
  Guillaume Chuard (Studio Ardworks), Lausanne / London

Typeface
  LL Geigy, Robert Huber / Lineto, Zurich

Photography (p. 7)
  © FOC / Diana Pfammatter

Translations
  Aurélie Duthoo (DE → FR)
  Silvia Giacomotti (DE/FR → IT)
  Lucas Moreno (IT → FR)
  Philippe Moser (FR / IT → DE)
  Mark O'Neil (FR → EN)
  Alain Perrinjaquet (DE → FR)
  Sarah Ponting (IT → EN)
  Annie Urselli (DE → IT)

Proofreading
  FOC Translation Services (DE / FR / IT)
  Mark O'Neil (EN)

Printing
  Gremper AG, Basel

Weitere Übersetzungen der Gespräche finden Sie auf:
Veuillez trouver les traductions françaises sur :
La traduzione italiana delle interviste è disponibile su:
www.schweizerkulturpreise.ch/design

© 2024 Federal Office of Culture, Bern and Verlag Scheidegger & Spiess AG, Zurich

Texts © the authors
Images © the artists

Verlag Scheidegger & Spiess
Niederdorfstrasse 54
8001 Zurich, Switzerland
www.scheidegger-spiess.ch

Scheidegger & Spiess is being supported by the Federal Office of Culture with a general subsidy for the years 2021–24.

All rights reserved; no part of this publication may be reproduced, stored in a retrieval system or transmitted in any form or by any means, electronic, mechanical, photocopying, recording, or otherwise, without the prior written consent of the publisher.

The three winners of the Swiss Grand Award for Design 2024 are: Paola De Martin, designer and design researcher, Lucie Meier, fashion designer and creative director, Luciano Rigolini, photographer and producer for auteur documentary film. The publication is distributed in a box containing three individual booklets – one for each winner – that are not available separately.

ISBN: 978-3-03942-207-4

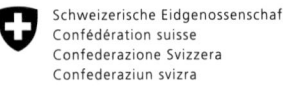

Schweizerische Eidgenossenschaft
Confédération suisse
Confederazione Svizzera
Confederaziun svizra

Eidgenössisches Departement des Innern EDI
Département fédéral de l'intérieur DFI
Dipartimento federale dell'interno DFI
Departament federal da l'intern DFI
Bundesamt für Kultur BAK
Office fédéral de la culture OFC
Ufficio federale della cultura UFC
Uffizi federal da cultura UFC

Schweizer Grand Prix Design

Grand Prix suisse de design   Gran Premio svizzero di design

Swiss Grand Award for Design

2024

Schweizer Grand Prix Design 2024

Der Schweizer Grand Prix Design zeichnet exemplarische Karrieren aus und bietet Sichtbarkeit für die Designschaffenden, deren Arbeit in der Sparte besonders interessante Wege und Gedankengänge eröffnet.

Welchen Stimmen wollen wir in einer Welt voller Lärm Gehör verschaffen? Sollen wir diejenigen würdigen, deren Arbeit dazu dient, unsere Objekte, Plakate, Webseiten oder Kleider schöner zu gestalten? Diejenigen, die sie nachhaltiger machen? Diejenigen, die Design als sozialen Akt verstehen? Kann Design überhaupt neue Botschaften vermitteln? Was bedeuten Denken und Kreieren im Jahr 2024, wenn die Welt in ihrer ganzen Vielfalt und Komplexität berücksichtigt wird?

Die Jury pflegt einen lebendigen Austausch zu diesen Fragen und misst der Botschaft, die sie mit der Wahl der Preisträgerinnen und Preisträger sendet, grösste Bedeutung bei. Es geht darum, die Arbeit von Einzelpersonen auszuzeichnen, die einen neuartigen, kreativen, engagierten Ansatz zur Anwendung bringen oder die Disziplin bedeutend geprägt haben und weiterhin prägen – selbstverständlich ohne dabei die Frauen zu vergessen, die besonders in der Vergangenheit weniger sichtbar waren. Ein Preis des Bundes, der von Kolleginnen und Kollegen aus der Sparte vergeben wird, würdigt auch Designschaffende, die die Grenzen ihrer Praxis ausloten.

2024 fiel die Wahl auf Persönlichkeiten, die in ihren Bereichen neue Wege beschreiten. Der Beitrag von Paola De Martin geht weit über die traditionelle Forschung hinaus. Mit ihren kritischen Betrachtungen bietet sie eine transdisziplinäre Herangehensweise an das Design, das sie in den gesellschaftlichen und politischen Kontext setzt. Bei ihr werden die Themen von Migration, Rassismus und gesellschaftlichem Ausschluss innerhalb der Disziplin betrachtet. Die Modedesignerin Lucie Meier hat in beeindruckender Geschwindigkeit international Karriere gemacht. Mit 40 Jahren arbeitet sie für grosse Häuser wie Louis Vuitton, Balenciaga, Dior oder Jil Sander. Wer seine Karriere im Ausland macht, erhält in der Schweiz oft spät Anerkennung. Mit Lucie Meier wollen wir eine Designerin würdigen, die über sichere und feine Kenntnisse ihres Handwerks verfügt. Luciano Rigolini hat mit seinen 74 Jahren nie damit aufgehört, die Bilder zu hinterfragen. Durch den Akt der Aneignung erforscht er sein Material und interessiert sich dabei besonders für triviale Fotografien, die unter seinem Blick neues plastisches Potenzial entfalten. Gleichzeitig verfolgte er eine internationale Karriere als Produzent von dokumentarischen Autorenfilmen.

Indem sie mit dem Schweizer Grand Prix Design 2024 Persönlichkeiten würdigt, die sich an unterschiedlichen Momenten ihres Berufslebens befinden und die alle ihren ganz eigenen Ansatz verfolgen, zeigt die Jury die vielen Perspektiven, die das Design eröffnet. Die Anerkennung für so verschiedene

Arbeitsweisen wie die von Paola De Martin, Lucie Meier und Luciano Rigolini unterstreicht die Vielfalt der möglichen Karrieren. Mit ihrer persönlichen Geschichte beweisen sie, dass es nicht nötig ist, einer Elite anzugehören, um Anerkennung zu erlangen. Denn die Grundsteine ihrer Kreativität sind Reflexion und Engagement.

Nathalie Herschdorfer, Präsidentin der Eidgenössischen Designkommission

Einleitung

Auch 18 Jahre nach der Lancierung der «höchsten Auszeichnung des Schweizer Designs» ist der Schweizer Grand Prix Design für das Bundesamt für Kultur (BAK) ein hervorragendes Instrument, um die Breite beruflicher Entwicklungswege und die Vielfalt im Design aufzuzeigen. Durch die Anerkennung unterschiedlicher Perspektiven und Herangehensweisen wird unser Blick auf die Bedeutung von Design in unserer Gesellschaft jedes Jahr reicher und dynamischer.

Der Preis wurde 2007 erstmals vergeben. Kurz davor wurden im BAK die «Projektbeiträge Design» eingestellt und die Eidgenössische Designkommission (EDnK) suchte nach neuen Wegen, die Designerinnen und Designer gezielter und proaktiver mit Fördergeldern zu unterstützen.

Im ersten Jahr wurden auf Vorschlag der EDnK fünf Preise vergeben, die von Beginn an mit je 40 000 Franken dotiert waren. Mit dem bedeutenden Schriftgestalter Adrian Frutiger und mit Bernhard Schobinger, einem der einflussreichsten Schmuckkünstler Europas, wurden international renommierte Persönlichkeiten ausgezeichnet. Mit der 1991 gegründeten Designagentur Nose, der Modedesignerin Ruth Grüninger und dem Grafiker Cornel Windlin, damals knapp 40-jährig, kam zudem eine jüngere Generation zum Zug. Ziel des BAK war es, Designschaffenden zu ermöglichen, an innovativen Projekten zu arbeiten und ihr kreatives Potenzial weiterzuentwickeln, ohne sich ausschliesslich auf den kommerziellen Erfolg konzentrieren zu müssen.

Die Auszeichnungen prägen ein Stück Schweizer Designgeschichte. Die dazu erscheinende Publikation beinhaltet oftmals erste Sichtungen von Archiven und dient als Basis für künftige Werkpräsentationen und Forschungsarbeiten. Gerade im vergangenen Jahr bekamen zahlreiche ehemalige Preisträgerinnen des Schweizer Grand Prix Design (SGPD) eine eigene Plattform: Im Landesmuseum war eine monografische Ausstellung über das Ausnahmetalent im Schweizer Modedesign Ursula Rodel (SGPD 2009) zu entdecken. Über die Leuchtendesign-Pionierin Rosmarie Baltensweiler (2019) erschien im letzten September ein umfangreicher Werkkatalog, Eleonore Peduzzi Riva (2023), die weit mehr als das weltberühmte DS-600-Sofa mitentwickelt hat, wurde an Panels eingeladen und mehrfach interviewt, im Museum für Gestaltung Zürich konnte man jüngst die textilen Wunderwerke von Claudia Caviezel (2016) geniessen und Sarah Kueng und Lovis Caputo (2020) erhielten Ende 2023 den wohlverdienten Goldenen Hasen von Hochparterre. Und aktuell freuen wir uns über eine Publikation mit zwölf neuen Alphabeten von Rosmarie Tissi (2018), die im Verlag About Books erscheint.

Die diesjährigen Preisträgerinnen Paola De Martin und Lucie Meier sowie den Preisträger Luciano Rigolini verbindet die Fähigkeit, Traditionen zu hinterfragen und neue Wege zu beschreiten. Wie die drei mit ihrem innovativen Schaffen dazu beitragen, Vielfalt, Inklusion, Ethik, Zusammenarbeit und Technologie in der Kultur zu fördern, können Sie, liebe Leserin, lieber Leser, nun bei der Lektüre erfahren. Ich wünsche Ihnen viele spannende Entdeckungen und wie jedes Jahr auch viel Inspiration für Ihre eigenen Projekte.

Anna Niederhäuser
Leitung Design
Bundesamt für Kultur

Grand Prix suisse de design 2024

Le Grand Prix suisse de design distingue des carrières exemplaires et offre une visibilité à des créatrices et des créateurs dont le travail ouvre une voie ou des réflexions particulièrement intéressantes dans ce domaine.

Quelles voix faire entendre dans un monde aussi bruyant que le nôtre ? Faut-il valoriser celles et ceux qui conçoivent des créations destinées à rendre nos objets, nos affiches, nos sites Internet, nos vêtements plus beaux ? Celles et ceux qui les rendent plus durables ? Celles et ceux qui voient dans le design un acte social ? Le design peut-il être porteur de nouveaux messages ? Que signifie, en 2024, penser et créer tout en tenant compte de la diversité et de la complexité de notre monde ?

Le jury échange activement autour de ces questions et considère avec la plus grande attention le message qu'il souhaite transmettre en distinguant trois lauréat-e-s. Il s'agit de valoriser le travail d'individus à l'approche novatrice, créatrice ou engagée, ou encore qui exercent ou qui ont exercé une influence marquante dans leur discipline. Ceci, bien sûr, sans oublier les femmes, qui dans le passé ont souvent été reléguées à l'arrière plan. L'annonce des Grands Prix attire l'attention des médias et permet de parler des différents domaines du design à un public varié. Un prix fédéral, décerné par des pairs, rend aussi hommage à des professionnels qui explorent les contours de leur pratique.

En 2024, le choix s'est porté sur des personnes qui ont choisi un chemin novateur dans leur domaine. La contribution de Paola De Martin dépasse largement la recherche traditionnelle. Par ses réflexions critiques, elle offre une approche transdisciplinaire au design qu'elle intègre dans un contexte social et politique. Chez elle, les questions de migration, de racisme et d'exclusion sociale s'invitent dans la discipline. La créatrice de mode Lucie Meier mène une carrière internationale fulgurante. À 40 ans, elle a travaillé pour de grandes maisons, parmi lesquelles Louis Vuitton, Balenciaga, Dior et Jil Sander. Pour celles et ceux qui développent une carrière à l'étranger, la reconnaissance arrive souvent de façon tardive. Avec Lucie Meier, il s'agit de valoriser une créatrice qui a de solides et sensibles connaissances dans son métier. Enfin, Luciano Rigolini est à 74 ans un créateur qui n'a jamais cessé d'interroger les images. C'est par l'acte d'appropriation qu'il explore sa matière, s'intéressant particulièrement aux photographies vernaculaires. Sous son regard, les photographies dévoilent de nouvelles potentialités plastiques. En parallèle il a mené une carrière internationale comme producteur dans le domaine du film documentaire d'auteur.

En réunissant autour du Grand Prix suisse de design 2024, des individus se trouvant à différents moments de leur vie professionnelle et qui témoignent chacun-e d'une approche singulière, le jury signifie que le design ouvre de nombreuses perspectives. Reconnaître le travail de Paola De Martin, de Lucie

Meier et de Luciano Rigolini dont les pratiques sont relativement éloignées l'une de l'autre, permet de montrer des voies multiples. À travers leur histoire personnelle, on voit qu'il n'est pas nécessaire d'appartenir à une élite pour aspirer à la reconnaissance, car le ciment de leur créativité réside dans la réflexion et l'engagement.

Nathalie Herschdorfer, Présidente de la Commission fédérale de design

Introduction

Dix-huit ans après la création de la « plus prestigieuse distinction du design suisse », le Grand Prix suisse de design de l'Office fédéral de la culture (OFC) demeure un remarquable instrument qui permet de mettre en évidence la diversité du design et celle des parcours professionnels dans le domaine. En reconnaissant des perspectives et des approches différentes, nous pouvons d'année en année porter un regard de plus en plus riche et dynamique sur l'importance du design dans notre société.

C'est en 2007 que le prix a été décerné pour la première fois. Peu de temps auparavant, l'OFC avait cessé d'octroyer ses « contributions à des projets de design » et la Commission fédérale de design était à la recherche de nouvelles manières de soutenir les designers par des aides ciblées et proactives.

La première année, cinq prix ont été décernés sur proposition de la CFD ; comme aujourd'hui, chacun d'eux était doté d'une somme de 40 000 francs. Ils couronnaient, d'une part, des personnalités de renommée internationale, comme Adrian Frutiger, important créateur de caractères d'imprimerie, et Bernhard Schobinger, un des plus influents bijoutiers d'art d'Europe. Mais ils faisaient aussi une place à la nouvelle génération, avec l'agence de design Nose, fondée en 1991, la créatrice de mode Ruth Grüninger et le graphiste Cornel Windlin, alors tout juste quarantenaire. Le but de l'OFC était de permettre à des designers de travailler à des projets novateurs et de développer leurs potentialités créatives sans qu'ils soient contraints de se concentrer sur le succès commercial.

Les prix décernés sont le reflet de tout un pan de l'histoire du design suisse. Souvent, la publication qui les accompagne donne un aperçu des archives des lauréats qui sera un point de départ pour des rétrospectives et des travaux de recherche ultérieurs. L'année dernière, nombre d'anciens lauréats du Grand Prix suisse de design ont été mis sur le devant de la scène. Le Musée national suisse a ainsi consacré une exposition monographique à Ursula Rodel (Grand Prix 2009), créatrice de mode d'un exceptionnel talent, tandis qu'un riche catalogue de l'œuvre de Rosmarie Baltensweiler (2019), pionnière du design de luminaires, paraissait en septembre dernier. Dans le même temps, Eleonore Peduzzi Riva (2023), dont le canapé DS-600, mondialement connu, n'est de loin pas la seule création, courait les tables rondes et les entretiens, et le Musée du design de Zurich accueillait les merveilleuses œuvres textiles de Claudia Caviezel (2016), alors que la revue Hochparterre attribuait à Sarah Kueng et Lovis Caputo (2020) une distinction amplement méritée, le Goldener Hase, et que, tout récemment, nous pouvions nous réjouir de la parution aux éditions About Books de douze nouveaux alphabets de Rosmarie Tissi (2018).

Les deux lauréates et le lauréat de cette année, Paola De Martin, Lucie Meier et Luciano Rigolini, s'apparentent par leur capacité de remettre en question les traditions et de s'engager dans de nouvelles voies. Dans les pages qui suivent, vous apprendrez comment ces trois créateurs innovants promeuvent une culture basée sur la diversité, l'inclusion, l'éthique, la coopération et la technologie. Je vous souhaite de faire des découvertes captivantes et d'y puiser, comme chaque année, une riche inspiration pour vos propres projets.

Anna Niederhäuser
Responsable design
Office fédéral de la culture

[IT → p. 43, EN → p. 45]

Luciano Rigolini

Luciano Rigolini

Das Bild hinterfragen

von Marco Franciolli

Die künstlerische Tätigkeit von Luciano Rigolini ist vielstimmig und umfasst die Fotografie, die Realisierung von Künstlerbüchern und die Produktion von dokumentarischen Autorenfilmen. Ein roter Faden zieht sich durch diese verschiedenen Ausdrucksformen, die sich ineinander verweben, sich gegenseitig bereichern und dabei auf originelle Weise ontologisch den Status des zeitgenössischen Bildes analysieren und dessen Beziehung zur Realität vertieft untersuchen. Die Relevanz seiner intensiven künstlerischen Tätigkeit, die inzwischen mehr als dreissig Jahre dauert, wird durch zahlreiche Preise und Auszeichnungen im Fotografie- und Filmbereich auf nationaler und internationaler Ebene bestätigt.

Rigolinis fotografisches Schaffen beginnt 1990 mit dem Zyklus *Paesaggi urbani*, dessen grossformatige Schwarz-Weiss-Bilder den Stadtraum aus einem eigenwilligen Blickwinkel zeigen, in dem die traditionelle perspektivische Sicht zugunsten einer geometrischen Komposition aufgegeben wird, die an die Stilmittel der konstruktivistischen Collage erinnert. Die kompositorische Zerteilung entsteht in diesen Bildern einzig aus der Wahl des Blickpunktes heraus, ohne jeglichen Eingriff in das Negativ oder den Druck. Die Serie *Paesaggi urbani* verfolgt Rigolini bis 2002 weiter, während er gleichzeitig einen kreativen Prozess durchläuft, der ihn dazu führt, immer mehr auf den physischen Akt des Fotografierens zu verzichten und stattdessen auf anonyme Aufnahmen zurückzugreifen. Der Künstler legt einen unerschöpflichen Bilderbestand an, indem er sich von anderen in unterschiedlichen Absichten und zu verschiedenen Zwecken geschaffene Fotografien aneignet, um sie nach seinem ästhetischen und konzeptuellen Programm zu überarbeiten und so zu seinen eigenen Werken zu machen. Ausgangspunkt für diese neue Schaffensrichtung ist eine Sammlung von Fotografien, die Rigolini während zehn Jahren zusammengestellt hat, um daraus sein Werk *What you see* entstehen zu lassen, das er 2008 an einer Ausstellung in der Fotostiftung Schweiz in Winterthur zeigte. Unter dem gleichen Titel verwirklicht er auch das erste seiner Bücher, die als eigenständige Kunstwerke zu verstehen sind. Parallel zu den fotografischen Zyklen schafft Rigolini seither regelmässig Künstlerbücher, in denen der stark konzeptuelle Charakter, der seiner gesamten künstlerischen Arbeit zugrunde liegt, besonders deutlich wird. Die Auswahl der Bilder, deren Abfolge und die grafische Komposition prägen ein neuartiges und eigenständiges Erzählen, das die ursprüngliche Bedeutung der Abbildungen hinter sich lässt. Im starken Drang zum Suchen und Sammeln von fotografischen Bildern in Archiven oder auch im Web zeigt sich ein grundlegendes Element von Rigolinis ästhetischem Diskurs: die Obsession für das Bild. Es sind dabei vor allem Fotografien aus Archiven des Maschinenbaus und der Automobilindustrie, die das Interesse des Künstlers wecken.

Die zwanzigjährige Erfahrung – seit 1995 – von Luciano Rigolini als Produzent von dokumentarischen Autorenfilmen für den französisch-deutschen Fernsehsender ARTE mit Sitz in Paris hat seine persönliche Forschung über den Status des Bildes zweifellos erweitert und bereichert. Die von ihm entworfene und geleitete Sendung «La Lucarne» bot dem experimentellen und unabhängigen Autorenfilm einen wichtigen Freiraum. In Rigolinis Jahren bei ARTE verfolgte er mit seiner Filmauswahl die Absicht, die Kunst in das Medium Fernsehen zu bringen. Daraus entwickelte er erfolgreiche Zusammenarbeiten mit den prägendsten Künstlerinnen und Künstlern, Regisseurinnen und Regisseuren der internationalen Filmszene. In seiner Tätigkeit als Dokumentarfilmemacher hatte Luciano Rigolini auch die Gelegenheit, sich mit den grundlegenden Fragen der ambivalenten Beziehung des Bildes zur Realität zu befassen – eine Auseinandersetzung, die in der Entwicklung seines fotografischen Schaffens und in seinen Büchern klar zu erkennen ist. Ein Beispiel dafür ist der Zyklus, den er Aufnahmen vom Mond aus dem NASA-Archiv zu den Apollo-Missionen 15 und 16 gewidmet hat. Rigolini vereint auf innovative Weise seine Leidenschaft für die Kunst- und Fotografiegeschichte mit den technischen Möglichkeiten des Digitaldrucks, um – ausgehend von wissenschaftlichen Aufnahmen, die ohne jeglichen ästhetischen Anspruch entstanden sind – neue Bilder zu erschaffen, mehrdeutige Werke auf der Schwebe zwischen malerischer und fotografischer Ästhetik. Der Künstler richtet dabei seine Aufmerksamkeit auf die Eigenschaft solcher Fotografien, unübliche Lesarten hervorzurufen. Es überrascht daher nicht, dass er sich auch für Aufnahmen von UFOs interessiert, von Flugobjekten, deren Abbildung einzig durch den Zweifel begründet ist. Die Drucke von analogen Aufnahmen aus einem Archiv für Ufologie überträgt der Künstler auf einen digitalen Bildträger und druckt sie grossformatig aus. Das Format verändert die Eigenschaft des Bildes und produziert so eine «Mise en abyme» des dargestellten Gegenstandes. Die

Bilder erschienen 2022 im Band *Inexcplicata Volantes* beim japanischen Verlag Akio Nagasawa.

In seiner jüngsten Schaffensphase beginnt Luciano Rigolini wiederum einen neuen kreativen Prozess mit Bildern, die mithilfe von Algorithmen der künstlichen Intelligenz generiert werden. Nachdem Rigolini aufgehört hat, eigene Bilder aufzunehmen, verzichtet er nun auch auf das Verwenden von anonymen Fotografien, um sich Bildern zu widmen, die anhand detaillierter Angaben des Künstlers von der künstlichen Intelligenz geliefert werden. In einem Zyklus von Bildern, die wie Aufnahmen von stillgelegten Industriebauten wirken, wird die immer durchlässiger werdende Grenze zwischen Malerei und Fotografie in Rigolinis Schaffen weiter aufgelöst. Durch die virtuelle Ausarbeitung von Formen, Farben und Strukturen bekräftigt der Künstler in aller Deutlichkeit, dass ein fotografisches Bild die Realität immer nur scheinbar wiedergibt.

Marco Franciolli kuratiert seit 1989 Ausstellungen und Publikationen zu Themen der modernen und zeitgenössischen Kunst, Fotografie und Architektur. Er war Direktor und Konservator des Museo Cantonale d'arte und der erste Direktor des Museo d'arte della Svizzera italiana MASI im Kulturzentrum LAC in Lugano. Seit 2018 ist er freischaffend als Kurator und Kunstkritiker tätig.

Luciano Rigolini

Interroger l'image

par Marco Franciolli

L'activité artistique de Luciano Rigolini se conjugue au pluriel: il est photographe, réalise des livres d'artistes et produit des films documentaires d'auteur. Un fil rouge unit ces modes d'expression, qui s'entrecroisent et s'enrichissent mutuellement en un parcours ontologique original visant à interroger le statut de l'image contemporaine, mais aussi à approfondir le rapport que le rendu visuel entretient avec la réalité. Son intense activité artistique s'étend sur plus de trente ans, et la quantité de récompenses et de prix de photographie et de cinéma qu'il a reçus, aussi bien sur le plan national qu'international, atteste de la pertinence de son travail.

En 1990, Rigolini débute son parcours de photographe par un cycle de clichés noir-blanc en grand format intitulé *Paesaggi urbani* (paysages urbains). L'artiste y adopte un point de vue particulier pour représenter l'espace urbain, une approche qui l'amène à déconstruire la vision perspectiviste traditionnelle au profit d'une composition géométrique rappelant les spécificités stylistiques du collage constructiviste. La composition, le découpage résultent ici uniquement du choix du point de vue, sans aucune manipulation du négatif ou de l'impression. Cette série se poursuit jusqu'en 2002, mais Rigolini entame en parallèle un parcours créatif qui le conduit à renoncer progressivement à l'acte physique de la prise de vue pour récupérer des instantanés d'auteurs anonymes. L'artiste met ainsi à contribution un fonds iconographique inépuisable, s'approprie des images réalisées par d'autres, avec des intentions et des finalités diverses, pour les retravailler selon son propre programme esthétique et conceptuel jusqu'à les transformer en œuvres personnelles. Le point de départ de cette nouvelle orientation créative est une collection de photographies récoltées pendant dix ans et assemblées pour former un travail original intitulé *What You See*, que Rigolini présente en 2008 lors d'une exposition à la Fondation suisse pour la photographie de Winterthour. Il produit par ailleurs un livre sous le même titre, le premier d'une série de volumes qui constituent en réalité des œuvres pleinement autonomes. En parallèle de ses cycles de photos, Rigolini réalise régulièrement des livres d'artistes qui réaffirment le caractère fortement conceptuel sous-jacent à toute sa production artistique: le choix des images, la séquence et la composition graphique déterminent une narration inédite et autonome qui transcende la valeur iconique originelle. Le besoin compulsif de rechercher et de collecter des vues photographiques dans les archives ou sur la Toile révèle un élément fondateur de son discours esthétique: l'obsession de l'image. Ce qui attire l'attention de l'artiste, ce sont principalement des photos issues d'archives de l'industrie mécanique et automobile.

Pendant vingt ans, de 1995 à 2015, Luciano Rigolini dirige en tant que producteur une case réservée aux films documentaires d'auteur sur ARTE, la chaîne de télévision culturelle franco-

allemande basée à Paris. Cette expérience a sans aucun doute contribué à élargir et enrichir ses recherches personnelles ultérieures autour du statut de l'image. L'émission *La Lucarne*, dont il a été le créateur et le directeur, a offert un espace de liberté extraordinaire au cinéma d'auteur, expérimental et indépendant. L'idéal qui a guidé les choix de Luciano Rigolini au fil des années passées chez ARTE a été celui de faire entrer l'art dans le média télévisuel, et c'est dans cette optique qu'il a développé des collaborations fructueuses avec des artistes et des réalisateurs parmi les plus influents et originaux de la scène cinématographique internationale. C'est également dans le cadre de son activité liée aux documentaires que Rigolini a pu se confronter aux questions de fond posées par le rapport ambigu qu'entretient l'image avec la réalité. Ces réflexions se reflètent clairement dans l'évolution de sa production d'œuvres photographiques et de livres. On en trouve un bon exemple dans son cycle de photos de la lune prises lors des missions Apollo 15 et Apollo 16, qu'il a trouvées dans les archives de la NASA. De manière inédite, Rigolini associe sa passion pour l'histoire de l'art et de la photo aux techniques d'impression numérique pour créer du nouveau à partir d'images scientifiques dépourvues de toute intention esthétique, des œuvres ambiguës porteuses d'une nature à la fois picturale et photographique. L'artiste concentre son attention sur cette propriété qu'a l'image photographique d'engendrer des parcours de lecture inhabituels ; dans ce sens, il n'est guère surprenant qu'il se soit intéressé aux clichés d'ovnis, ces objets volants dont l'image n'est rendue plausible qu'au travers du doute. Pour son ouvrage *Inexplicata Volantes*, publié en 2022 par l'éditeur japonais Akio Nagasawa, Rigolini a transposé en numérique des tirages de clichés analogiques issus d'archives ufologiques avant de les imprimer en grand format, modifiant ainsi la nature même des images et provoquant une mise en abyme de la thématique.

Dans sa phase la plus récente, Rigolini entame un nouveau parcours créatif en générant des images à l'aide d'algorithmes : après avoir renoncé à la prise de vue pour utiliser des photos anonymes, l'artiste passe désormais à la production d'images sur la base d'indications très détaillées fournies à une intelligence artificielle. La frontière entre la nature photographique et picturale des œuvres de Luciano Rigolini, qui s'estompe progressivement au fil des années, devient encore plus floue dans un de ses récents travaux : un cycle d'images qui semblent être des instantanés d'architectures industrielles désaffectées. En réalité, à travers l'élaboration virtuelle des formes, des couleurs et des structures, l'artiste affirme sans équivoque que l'image photographique est toujours, et seulement, un simulacre de la réalité.

Marco Franciolli est commissaire d'exposition et de publications sur l'art moderne et contemporain, la photographie et l'architecture depuis 1989. Il a été directeur-conservateur du Musée cantonal d'art de Lugano et premier directeur du Musée d'art de la Suisse italienne (MASI). Depuis 2018, il travaille en tant que curateur et critique d'art indépendant.

[IT → p. 37, EN → p. 38]

A

B, C

D, E

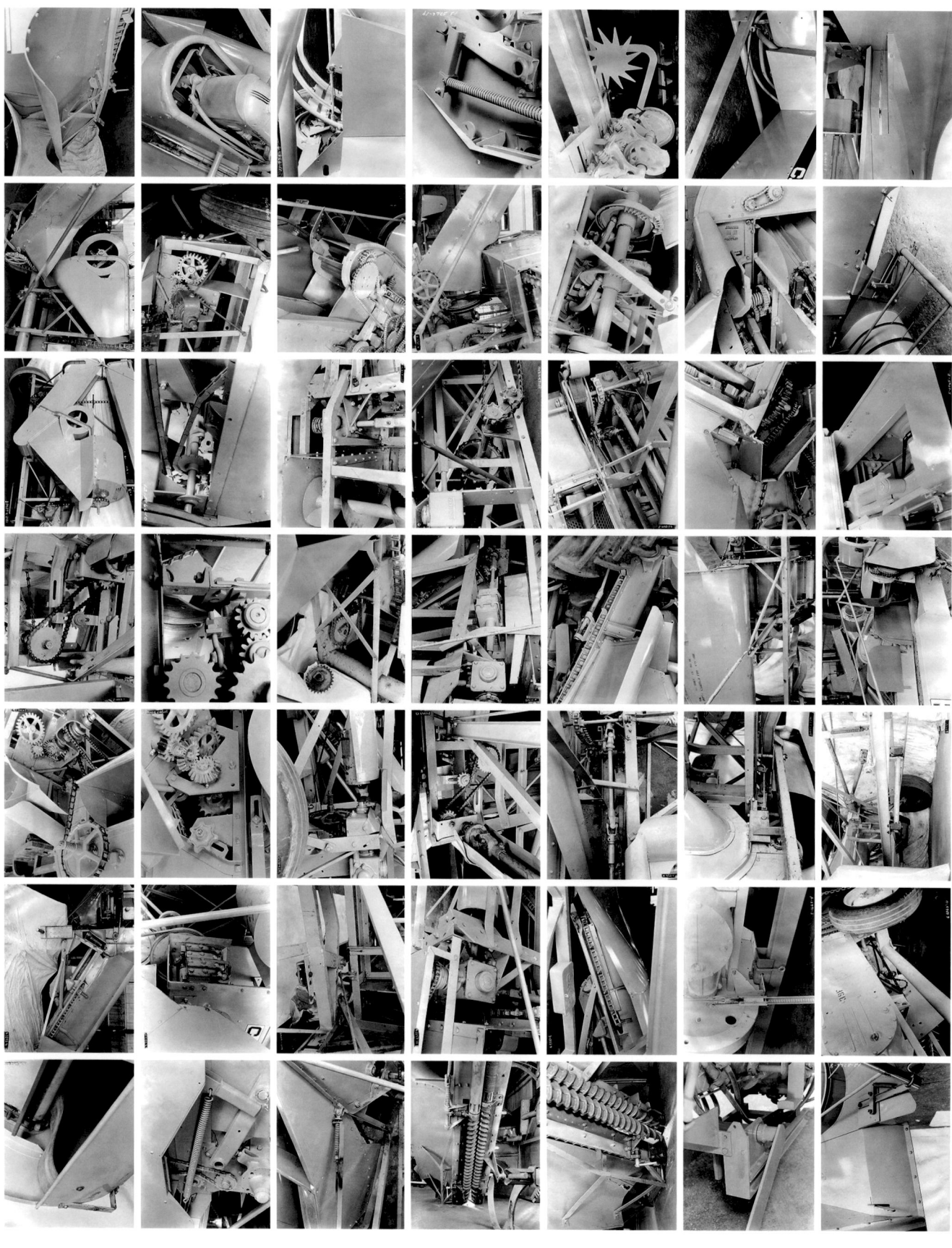
F

A. *Urban Landscapes* (selection), 1990–2002, 124 × 124 cm each. Private collections
B. *Cuts*, 2, 2021, Fine art inkjet print, 70 × 90 cm. Fotostiftung Schweiz collection
C. *Cuts*, 4, 2021, Fine art inkjet print, 70 × 90 cm. Fotostiftung Schweiz collection
D. *Doors*, 2012, diptych, 150 × 125 cm each. Photo Élysée collection, Lausanne
E. *Car interior*, 2020, diptych, 172 × 147 cm each. Private collection
F. *Mechanics*, 2017, set of 49 vintage prints, 200 × 150 cm. Artist's collection
G. *Ufo*, 2023, AI-generated images, Fine art inkjet print, 50 × 50 cm each. Artist's collection
H. *Moonscape A1-A2*, 2015, diptych, 120 × 120 cm each, rereading of NASA images. Private collection
I. *Still life*, 2007, industrial image, Fine art inkjet print, 106 × 271 cm, m.a.x. museo collection, Chiasso
J. *Architectures* (selection), 2024, AI-generated images, 20 × 20 cm each. Artist's collection

[IT] MARCO FRANCIOLLI IN CONVERSAZIONE CON LUCIANO RIGOLINI, 18 GENNAIO 2024

Marco Franciolli: Il tuo è un percorso creativo esteso su oltre trent'anni, in un periodo a cavallo fra due secoli segnato da profondi mutamenti in ambito culturale, artistico e tecnologico. Questa nostra conversazione offre l'occasione per alcune considerazioni sulla fotografia e sul tuo rapporto con l'immagine.

Luciano Rigolini: In effetti le peculiarità culturali e artistiche dell'epoca nella quale si è svolta – e tuttora si svolge – la mia attività creativa hanno inciso in modo molto significativo sul mio rapporto con l'immagine e con la fotografia. Per me rimangono imprescindibili i riferimenti alle avanguardie artistiche del Novecento, in primis il Bauhaus e il Costruttivismo, ma anche l'arte concettuale e quella minimalista che hanno impregnato gli anni della mia formazione e hanno plasmato in modo indelebile la mia dimensione estetica. A guidare la mia ricerca sono state però soprattutto le questioni relative allo statuto stesso della fotografia, e in questo senso il cambiamento intervenuto a fine anni Ottanta del secolo scorso, con l'entrata della fotografia nei musei e nell'arte contemporanea, ha determinato una ridefinizione dell'estetica e della pratica fotografica. Due protagonisti di questo rinnovamento sono stati indubbiamente i fotografi tedeschi della Nuova Oggettività Bernd e Hilla Becher. Il loro approccio concettuale al documento fotografico rimane per me un riferimento irrinunciabile. Infine, l'avvento del digitale ha rappresentato un vero e proprio mutamento epocale nella definizione di cosa sia la fotografia e ha aperto inedite possibilità, che mi hanno portato a voler indagare nuovi percorsi e nuove immagini.

MF: Qual è stata la tua prima fotografia?

LR: Ho un ricordo molto preciso, a quattordici anni ho ricevuto in prestito da mio padre il primo apparecchio fotografico, una vecchia Zeiss Ikon, 6 × 6, a soffietto. Inserito il rullino nel caricatore, ho iniziato a scattare dei ritratti a un'amica. Nella foga e nell'entusiasmo del momento ho però dimenticato di far avanzare il film e così mi sono ritrovato con una strana immagine, frutto della sovrapposizione dei diversi scatti. La natura misteriosa e affascinante di quella immagine stratificata è stata una vera rivelazione e ha probabilmente contribuito alla mia passione per la fotografia. Ho infatti scoperto in quel momento l'autonomia dell'immagine fotografica rispetto alla realtà.

MF: Nel 1990 hai dato avvio al ciclo fotografico *Paesaggi urbani*, fotografie in bianco e nero di grande formato, 124 × 124 cm, che ritraggono dettagli di contesti urbani e di architetture. Fin da questi primi lavori è evidente una rilettura della realtà in chiave costruttivista. Qual è la genesi di queste immagini?

LR: *Ad interessarmi era la possibilità di scardinare la visione prospettica attraverso la scelta del punto di vista. Infatti, non ho manipolato in alcun modo l'immagine né in fase di ripresa né al momento della stampa. Ho piuttosto riorganizzato le forme secondo una logica geometrizzante attraverso il mio punto di vista, inevitabilmente denso di riferimenti alle avanguardie, in particolare ai collage costruttivisti. Il lavoro sulle città ha avuto un immediato riscontro da parte delle istituzioni museali e del milieu fotografico, con mostre al Museo Cantonale d'Arte a Lugano e al Kunsthaus di Zurigo e nel 1993 ho realizzato il portfolio Città aperta/Open City per la Rice University di Houston, dove ero stato invitato a tenere dei corsi sul rapporto fra fotografia e architettura.*

MF: Negli stessi anni ha inizio l'avventura presso ARTE, a Parigi, nell'ambito della produzione di film documentari d'autore. Come si è presentata questa opportunità, rivelatasi così determinante per il tuo percorso?

LR: All'inizio degli anni Ottanta ho compiuto studi di cinema a Parigi, all'Université Paris VIII, dove ho avuto la fortuna di poter seguire i corsi del grande filosofo Gilles Deleuze, che stava preparando il suo libro culto *Cinéma. Vol 1. L'image-mouvement*. Per me sono stati anni fondamen-

1. Luciano Rigolini in New York, shooting a documentary with his Arriflex camera in the 1970s.

> «Ad interessarmi era la possibilità di scardinare la visione prospettica attraverso la scelta del *punto di vista*».

tali dal punto di vista della formazione culturale, ma anche della realizzazione personale, al punto che la Francia è divenuta la mia patria d'adozione. Nel 1995 Thierry Garrel, che dirigeva l'unità dei programmi documentari della televisione culturale europea ARTE a Parigi, dopo aver visto i miei film in vari festival, mi ha proposto la produzione di una trasmissione di documentari di società per un anno. All'epoca lavoravo come regista per la televisione Svizzera e naturalmente la proposta di poter lavorare a Parigi per un canale televisivo culturale e sperimentale era entusiasmante. L'avventura, però, non si è limitata a un anno, ma è durata per un ventennio, dal 1995 al 2015.

Marco Franciolli: Your creative journey spans a period of over thirty years, straddling two centuries and marked by profound changes in the spheres of art, culture and technology. Our conversation offers the opportunity to reflect on photography and your relationship with the image.

Luciano Rigolini: Indeed, the cultural and artistic hallmarks of the era in which my creative activity took and continues to take place have had a huge impact on my relationship with the image and photography. The references to the 20th-century avant-gardes remain inescapable for me, first and foremost Bauhaus and Constructivism, but also Conceptualism and Minimalism, which permeated my formative years and indelibly shaped my aesthetic dimension. What guided my work, however, were primarily issues regarding the status of photography, and in this sense the change that occurred when photography entered art and contemporary art museums at the end of the 1980s resulted in a redefinition of photographic aesthetics and practice. The German photographers of the New Objectivity movement Bernd and Hilla Becher were undoubtedly two key figures in this process. Their conceptual approach to the photographic document remains an essential touchstone for me. Finally, the advent of the digital age was a real game-changer in defining what photography is and opened up new possibilities, which made me want to explore new paths and images.

2. L'Image-Mouvement course by the philosopher Gilles Deleuze, Paris VIII University, 1982. Photo: unknown

MF: What was your first photograph?

LR: I have a very clear memory of it. When I was fourteen, my father lent me my first camera, an old 6 × 6 Zeiss Ikon with bellows. After loading the film, I started to take portraits of a friend. However, in the heat and enthusiasm of the moment, I forgot to wind the film on and thus ended up with a strange image, which was the result of superimposing several shots. The mysterious and fascinating nature of that layered image was a true revelation and probably contributed to my passion for photography. Indeed, it was in that moment that I discovered the autonomy of the photographic image in relation to reality.

"What interested me was the possibility to disrupt perspective through the choice of viewpoint."

MF: In 1990 you commenced the photographic cycle *Paesaggi urbani* (Urban Landscapes): large-format (124 × 124 cm) black-and-white photographs portraying details of urban environments and architecture. A constructivist reinterpretation of reality is apparent from these early works. What is the origin of these images?

LR: What interested me was the possibility to disrupt perspective through the choice of viewpoint. In fact, I did not manipulate the image in any way, either during shooting or printing. Rather, I reorganised the forms according to a geometric logic from my own viewpoint, inevitably packed with references to the avant-gardes, and particularly to constructivist collages. My work on cities garnered an immediate response from museums and the photographic community, with exhibitions at the Museo Cantonale d'Arte in Lugano and the Kunsthaus in Zurich, and in 1993 I created the portfolio Città aperta/Open City for Rice University in Houston, where I had been invited to teach courses on the relationship between photography and architecture.

MF: The same period marked the beginning of your adventure at ARTE in Paris, producing creative and auteur documentary films. How did this opportunity, which proved so crucial for your career, arise?

3. Opening of the exhibition *Zürich – Ein Fotoportrait*, at Kunsthaus Zürich, 1997, Luciano Rigolini with Giorgio von Arb, Lewis Baltz, Martin Parr and Paul Graham (fltr). Photo: unknown

LR: In the early 1980s I studied film at Paris 8 University, where I was lucky enough to be able to attend courses held by the great philosopher Gilles Deleuze, who was writing his cult book *Cinema 1: The Movement Image*. This was a crucial time for me in terms of cultural education, but also regarding personal fulfilment, to the point that France became my adopted homeland. In 1995, after having seen my films at various festivals, Thierry Garrel, head of the documentary unit of the European cultural television channel ARTE in Paris, offered me the production of a documentary programme for a year. At the time I was working as a director for Swiss television and naturally the offer to work in Paris for a cultural and experimental television channel was exciting. However, the adventure was not limited to a year, but continued for twenty, from 1995 to 2015.

MF: Twenty years is a very long time in career and creative terms. What interested you in this experience and what did it give you?

MF: Vent'anni sono un lasso di tempo molto importante nel percorso di lavoro e creativo. Cosa ti ha interessato in questa esperienza e cosa ti ha dato?

LR: Ad ARTE France mi è stato offerto in seguito uno spazio di libertà straordinaria con *La Lucarne*, una trasmissione nuova, da ideare e sviluppare, interamente affidata a me, che nel corso degli anni è diventata un riferimento per i cineasti del mondo intero. A guidarmi è stato il desiderio e la convinzione di poter realizzare un'utopia, quella cioè di portare l'arte e la creazione dentro il mezzo televisivo. *La Lucarne* è diventata un vero laboratorio di produzione di prototipi rispetto agli stereotipi del linguaggio televisivo. Spazi di autentica sperimentazione, che oggi purtroppo non esistono più. Parallelamente ho potuto anche ideare la collezione *Photo*, un'opera monumentale costituita da 12 film e pubblicata nel 2012, sulla storia della fotografia dalle origini ai nostri giorni, realizzata con la consulenza scientifica di Quentin Bajac, già Head Curator per la fotografia del MoMA.

MF: Quali sono stati gli incontri e le collaborazioni più marcanti negli anni passati ad ARTE?

LR: Durante i vent'anni di creazione come produttore ho incontrato cineasti che hanno lasciato in me un segno indelebile sia sul piano artistico sia su quello umano. Ho sempre avuto un ruolo attivo nel ricercare artisti e cineasti che si distinguessero per le loro opere radicali. Non solo figure affermate, ma anche giovani cineasti in divenire. Con alcuni di loro nel corso degli anni ho stretto profondi legami di amicizia. Da sempre avevo il desiderio di lavorare con Laurie Anderson. L'ho chiamata a New York dandole carta bianca, ma per mesi aveva difficoltà a trovare il soggetto. Ci siamo allora incontrati a Parigi, c'era anche suo marito Lou Reed; erano ancora traumatizzati per la perdita del loro cane, Lolabelle. Le ho quindi suggerito di sviluppare la sua visione della vita e della morte a partire dal legame con il cane appena scomparso. È nato così il suo primo film, *Heart of a dog* (2015), un capolavoro presentato in competizione alla Mostra

«A guidarmi è stato il desiderio e la convinzione di poter realizzare un'utopia, quella cioè di portare l'arte e la creazione dentro il mezzo televisivo».

del cinema di Venezia che ha avuto una carriera internazionale. Da allora ci incontriamo regolarmente, a New York o quando viene in Europa, e discutiamo dei suoi nuovi progetti e della vita.

L'incontro con Alain Cavalier mi ha cambiato la vita. Una grande figura del cinema francese, che ha lavorato tra gli altri con Alain Delon e Catherine Deneuve e ha lasciato l'industria del cinema ormai da molti anni, mosso dal desiderio di libertà creativa. Oggi, all'età di 92 anni, crea opere sperimentali intime e sublimi, lavorando con la semplicità della videocamera amatoriale; queste opere sono selezionate nei maggiori festival internazionali. Con lui, ad esempio, ho prodotto un saggio profondamente spirituale, *Lieux saints*, girato interamente all'interno di toilette pubbliche e private, luoghi, a suo dire, dove l'individuo è solo con se stesso. Da allora è nata un'amicizia che si è consolidata nel corso degli anni; ho una grande ammirazione, oltre che per la sua opera cinematografica, per la sua giovinezza di spirito e di pensiero.

Un'altra figura importante è quella della cineasta giapponese Naomi Kawase, che ho accompagnato fin dai suoi esordi, quando ancora non era conosciuta. Con lei ho prodotto i suoi primi film, autobiografici, poi in seguito è diventata una star internazionale, ospite regolare del Festival di Cannes. Ciononostante, il nostro legame d'amicizia continua tuttora e mi ha invitato in Giappone in qualità di presidente di giuria del suo festival del film a Nara. Naturalmente gli incontri importanti sono stati numerosi e potrei continuare citando anche il mitico Chris Marker, Chantal Akerman, Agnès Varda, Wang Bing, Tsai Mingliang, e tanti altri.

MF: Immagine fotografica e immagine in movimento presentano qualità estetiche molto differenti, come si conciliano nel tuo percorso creativo?

LR: Per me sono assolutamente complementari, nel senso che mi permettono di conciliare due assi di ricerca molto diversi. Nella fotografia è per me irrinunciabile la dimensione della massima oggettività. La rinuncia alla presenza della figura umana nelle mie immagini equivale al rifiuto di qualsiasi componente psicologica e/o sociologica. Come ho già citato in precedenza, la lezione radicale di Bernd e Hilla Becher è fondamentale nel rapporto con la realtà. Al tempo stesso, come chiarito in modo esemplare da Joseph Kosuth nella sua opera *One and Three Chairs* del 1965, l'oggetto sedia, la sua immagine e la sua definizione nel dizionario non sono la stessa cosa; la fotografia presenta una natura ambigua nella relazione con il reale che viene esemplificata concettualmente nell'opera di Kosuth. La mia ricerca fotografica interroga lo statuto della fotografia secondo gli stessi parametri concettuali. L'immagine in movimento, per contro, determina una possibilità di narrazione nella quale trovano spazio gli elementi spirituali, emozionali ed esistenziali della dimensione umana.

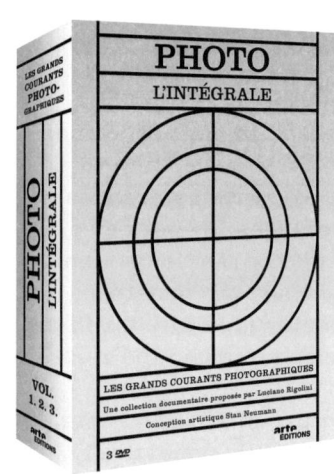

4. *Collection Photo*: 3-DVD box set with 12 films on the history of photography, conceived by Luciano Rigolini for ARTE, 2012

MF: Torniamo alla fotografia, dopo il ciclo dedicato alle città interviene un cambiamento significativo nel tuo rapporto con il mezzo: la progressiva rinuncia allo scatto fotografico a favore del recupero e dell'appropriazione di immagini realizzate da anonimi.

LR: At ARTE-France I was subsequently offered extraordinary freedom with *La Lucarne*, a new programme I was able to devise and develop. It was entirely entrusted to me and over the years become a touchstone for filmmakers throughout the world. I was guided by the desire and conviction that I could realise the utopia of bringing art and creation into the medium of television. *La Lucarne* became a veritable workshop for the production of prototypes with respect to the stereotypes of television language. It offered spaces for genuine experimentation, which unfortunately no longer exist today. At the same time, I was able to develop the *Photo* collection, a monumental work, published in 2012, consisting of 12 films on the history of photography from its origins to the present day, produced with the scientific collaboration of Quentin Bajac, former Chief Curator of Photography at MoMA.

MF: What were the most significant encounters and collaborations during the years you spent at ARTE?

LR: During my 20 creative years in production, I've met filmmakers, who have made a lasting impression on me on both an artistic and a human level. I have always played an active role in seeking out artists and filmmakers who stand out for their radical works. Not just established figures, but also young up-and-coming filmmakers, with some of whom I have forged close friendships over the years. I had always wanted to work with Laurie Anderson. I called her in New York, offering her carte blanche, but for months she had difficulty finding a subject. We then met in Paris; her husband Lou Reed was there too, and they were still traumatised by the loss of their dog, Lolabelle. So I suggested that she develop her view of life and death commencing with her bond with the dog she'd just lost. The result was her first film, *Heart of a Dog* (2015), a masterpiece presented at the Venice Film Festival, which went on to become an international success. Since then, we have been meeting regularly, in New York or when she comes to Europe, to talk about her new projects and life.

Meeting Alain Cavalier changed my life. He is a huge figure of French cinema, who worked with Alain Delon and Catherine Deneuve among others, and left the film industry many years ago, driven by a desire for creative freedom. Today, at the age of 92, he uses a simple amateur video camera to create intimate and sublime experimental works, which have been selected at major international festivals. With him, for example, I produced a deeply spiritual essay, *Lieux saints* (2007), filmed entirely inside public and private toilets, places where he maintains individuals are alone with themselves. It marked the beginning of a friendship, which has been consolidated over the years. I greatly admire not only his film work, but also his youthful spirit and way of thinking. Another important figure is the Japanese filmmaker Naomi Kawase, whom I have accompanied since her beginnings, when she was still unknown. I produced her first, autobiographical films with her, then she became an international star and a regular guest at the Cannes Film Festival. Our friendship nonetheless continues to this day, and she has invited me to Japan as president of the jury at her film festival in Nara. Of course, there have been numerous important encounters, and I could go on to mention the legendary Chris Marker, Chantal Akerman, Agnès Varda, Wang Bing, Tsai Ming-liang and many others.

MF: Photographic and moving images have very different aesthetic qualities, how are they compatible in your creative journey?

LR: In my opinion, they are absolutely complementary in the sense that they allow me to reconcile two very different research approaches. I consider maximum objectivity to be an essential dimension in photography; the absence of human figures in my images corresponds to the rejection of any kind of psychological and/or sociological component. As I mentioned earlier, Bernd and Hilla Becher's radical lesson is fundamental in the relationship with reality. At the same time, as Joseph Kosuth made abundantly clear in his 1965 work *One and Three Chairs*, a chair is not the same thing as its image nor its dictionary definition; photography is ambiguous

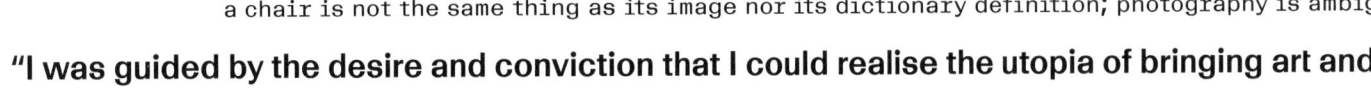

5. Poster created by the graphic designer Bruno Monguzzi for the first solo exhibition *Luciano Rigolini. Fotografie '90–'92* at the Museo Cantonale d'Arte, Lugano 1992, cover

6. Working session on *Cuts Series*, in Luciano Rigolini's studio, 2021. Photo: Luciano Rigolini archive

"I was guided by the desire and conviction that I could realise the utopia of bringing art and creation into the medium of television."

in its relationship with the reality that is conceptually exemplified in Kosuth's work. My photographic exploration probes the nature of the medium using the same conceptual parameters. The moving image, on the other hand, establishes a narrative possibility in which there is space for the spiritual, emotional and existential elements of the human dimension.

MF: To get back to photography, after the cities cycle, there was a significant change in your relationship with the medium, as you gradually stopped taking photographs, preferring instead to retrieve and appropriate images by anonymous photographers.

LR: Yes, my choice not to take photographs reflects what I told you in my previous answer. In this

7.

8.

9.

10.

11.

12.

13.

14.

7. L.R. at the Taiwan International Documentary Festival, Taipei, 2002
8. L.R., jury president at Nara International Film Festival (JP), 2014
9. L.R. with Wang Bing and the production team of the film *Ku Quian* at the Venice Film Festival 2016
10. L.R. with Wang Bing, Pardo d'oro for the film *Mrs. Fang*, Locarno Film Festival 2017
11. L.R. with Jacqueline Burckhardt, unknown, Sophie Calle and Laurie Anderson at the film premiere of *Heart of a Dog* of Laurie Anderson (fltr.), 72nd Venice Film Festival, 2015
12. Invitation for the film premiere of *Chats perchés* by Chris Marker at Centre Pompidou, Paris, 2004
13. L.R. with Laurie Anderson in her studio in New York, discovering a virtual reality project, 2018
14. L.R. with Laurie Anderson at the Rencontres de la Photographie, Arles, 2023. Photo: Jacqueline Burckhardt
15. L.R. with Naomi Kawase in Paris, 2023

PRIX ENSEMBLE DE L'ŒUVRE 1996 LIEUX SAINTS Alain Cavalier / Les Films de l'Astrophore
SUR LA PISTE Julien Samani / Château-Rouge Production
LE MONOLOGUE DE LA MUETTE Khady Sylla / Charlie Van Damme / Athenaise
LES BÉQUILLES DU LAMA YAPO Jowan Le Besco / Sangsho
LE CERCLE DES NOYÉS Pierre-Yves Vandeweerd / Oumar Ba Fara / Cobra Films
KAZAKHSTAN NAISSANCE D'UNE NATION Christian Barani / Guillaume Reynard / Atopic
ÉTOILE 2009 NO PASARAN, ALBUM SOUVENIR Henri-François Imbert / Libre Cours
LA VIE AILLEURS David Teboul / Les Films d'Ici
HARUKI YUKIMURA ET NANA CHAN Xavier Brillat / Arte France Développement
ASYLUM Catherine Bernstein / Paris Brest Productions
BRÈVES HISTOIRES DE L'AMOUR QUI DURE Florence Mauro / Zadig Productions
LES HÉRITIERS Eugenio Polgovsky / Arte France Développement
BROUILLON D'UN RÊVE 2007 HORS SAISON Jean-Claude Cottet / Petit à Petit Productions
VULNÉRABLE (AVANT DE PARTIR) Reine Mitri / Djinn House Productions
LE JOURNAL D'ESTHER Esther Gerber / Antoine Tracou / Amip Production
LE TESTAMENT AMOUREUX DE NEL André Dartevelle / Halolalune
KOYAMARU L'HIVER ET LE PRINTEMPS Jean-Michel Alberola / Mirage Illimité
KOYAMARU L'ÉTÉ ET L'AUTOMNE Jean-Michel Alberola / Mirage Illimité
ÉTOILE 2011 - BROUILLON D'UN RÊVE 2008 LE PLEIN PAYS Antoine Boutet / Red Star Cinema
ÉTOILE 2012 TERRITOIRE PERDU Pierre-Yves Vandeweerd / Cobra Films
THE CAMBODGIAN ROOM - LA CHAMBRE CAMBODGIENNE Giuseppe Schillaci / Tommaso Lusena de Sarmiento / Kolam
THEMERSON & THEMERSON Victoria Szymanska / Régie Plus
THEMERSON & THEMERSON Victoria Szymanska / 24 Images Production
POUSSIÈRE D'AMÉRIQUE Arnaud des Pallières / Les Films Hatari
EXERCICES DE DISPARITION Claudio Pazienza / Komplot Spel / Quark Productions
PHOTOGRAPHIC MEMORY Marie-Emmanuelle Hartness / Ross Mcelwee / French Connection Films
ÉTOILE 2013 MONSIEUR M, 1968 Laurent Cibien / Isabelle Berteletti / Lardux Films
BIELUTINE - DANS LE JARDIN DU TEMPS Clément Cogitore / Seppia
L'ÉTÉ DE GIANOCO Alessandro Comodin / Les Films d'Ici
JAURÈS Vincent Dieutre / La Huit Production
SEULES DANS LES MONTAGNES DU YUNNAN Bing Wang / Album Productions
NIGHT REPLAY Eléonore Weber / Patricia Allio / Atopic
BROUILLON D'UN RÊVE 2010 MON MUR À MOI Silvia Staderoli / Picofilms
PLIÈRES Pedro Gonzalez Rubio / Nara International Film Festival Organizing Commit
PIATTAFORMA LUNA Yuri Ancarani / Studio Ancarani
DA VINCI Yuri Ancarani / Studio Ancarani
PÈRE ET FILS Pawel Lozinski / Arte GEIE / TVP / Autoproduction
PRIX DE L'ŒUVRE DE L'ANNÉE 2015 / BROUILLON D'UN RÊVE 2011 LES TOURMENTES Pierre-Yves Vandeweerd / Zeugma Films
LE CIEL D'ANDREA Natacha-Suzanne Nisic / Seconde Vague
ÉTOILE 2015 QUAND JE SERAI DICTATEUR Yaël André / Morituri
ÉTOILE 2015 EAU ARGENTÉE, SYRIE AUTOPORTRAIT Ossama Mohammed / Wiam Simav Bedirxan / Les Films d'Ici
THE STORM MAKERS, CEUX QUI AMÈNENT LA TEMPÊTE Guillaume Petit / Phally Ngoeum / Tipasa Production / Bophana
ICAROS Pedro Gonzalez Rubio / Atopic
CHÈRE HUMAINE Stéphane Breton / Quark Productions
BROUILLON D'UN RÊVE 2006 LES YATZKAN Anna-Celia Kendall / Idéale Audience / Arte France

Scam*
*Société civile des auteurs multimédia

Liste des œuvres diffusées dans La Lucarne et déclarées à la Scam.

a selection of films produced by Luciano Rigolini for ARTE (facsimile)

MERCI LUCIANO RIGOLINI, LONGUE VIE À LA LUCARNE SUR ARTE

À LA RECHERCHE DE VERA BAADER / Danielle Jaggi / Videomontages
LA QUATRIÈME GÉNÉRATION / François Caillat / Gloria Films
JEAN ROUCH : TRAVERSÉE DE L'ŒUVRE 1995 ROUCH À L'ENVERS / Manthia Diawara / Jean Rouch / Manthia Diawara / Formation Films
CERCLE DE VIE / Yasha Aginsky / World Life
BIG ONE BYE BYE ONE / Alessandro Rossetto
SEULE - ODNA / Dmitry Kabakov / Dmitry Kabakov
RETOUR À ALEP / Marie Seurat / Éditions du Seuil / MP Production
PETITE CONVERSATION FAMILIALE / Hélène Lapiower / Margot Communication
NIGER - NOUVELLES IMPRESSIONS D'AFRIQUE / Jean-André Fieschi / Amip Production
PRIX DE L'ŒUVRE DE L'ANNÉE 2002 THE BOOT FACTORY / Lech Kowalski / Marc Andreani
CHIUSURA (FERMETURE DÉFINITIVE) / Alessandro Rossetto / Fandango
BONNE NOUVELLE / Vincent Dieutre / Movimento Productions
VASSILIS ALEXAKIS D'UNE LANGUE À L'AUTRE / Variety Moszynski / Francine Raymond / Jean-Michel Mariou / Les Films à Lou
PRIX DÉCOUVERTE 2003 / BROUILLON D'UN RÊVE 1999 COMME JE LA VOIS / Karine de Villers / Simple Productions
DISNEYLAND MON VIEUX PAYS NATAL / Arnaud des Pallières / Les Films d'ici
CHAMBRE DE BONNE / Maija-Lene Rettig / Les Films du Village
AUGUST AVANT L'EXPLOSION / UN ÉTÉ POURRI / Avi Mograbi / Les Films d'ici
PALESTINE TRIESTINE / Dominique Dubosc / Les Films d'ici
BROUILLON D'UN RÊVE 1999 DOR DE THE UNE HISTOIRE DE 1944 / Mireille Abramovici / Les Films d'ici
UNE AUTRE AMÉRIQUE / Neil Hollander / Zero Film GMBH
FEU MA MÈRE / Sandrine Dryvers / Thierry Tirtiaux / Dérives
ON HITLER'S HIGHWAY / Lech Kowalski / Agat Films & Compagnie
L'ATELIER D'ANDRÉ BRETON - L'OEIL À L'ÉTAT SAUVAGE / Fabrice François Maze / Seven Doc
DO YOU REMEMBER LAURIE ZIMMER ? / LAURA DISPARUE RETROUVÉE / Charlotte Szlovak / Zeugma Films
PRIX ENSEMBLE DE L'ŒUVRE 1995 ON THE TOU / Marianne Gosset / Les Films d'ici
ENSBRGEWERKE (SEEHAUSGMAN) / Bettina Clasen / Films à trois
L'AFFAIRE VALÉRIE / François Caillat / Archipels 33 / Ina
CARS ÉTRANGER / Sophie Bredier / Ex Nihilo / Ina
PRIX ENSEMBLE DE L'ŒUVRE 1992 CHRIS MARKER'S / Chris Marker / Les Films du jeudi
LA VIE DES ENFANTS AU XXIE SIÈCLE / ET COMMENT VONT LES ENFANTS / Babacar Sow / La Fabrique
BANJI (LES BANI) / David Teboul / Les Films d'ici
PARIS MARSEILLE / Sebastian Martinez Pineiro / Zorn Production International
PICK-UP - COSTA BLANCA, SOLEIL COUCHANT / Lucia Sanchez / Local Films
EN CO SIÈGE AVEC LES CAMARADES / Ulrike Knorr / Cobra Films / Majade Films
UNE FENÊTRE OUVERTE / Khady Sylla / Charlie Van Damme / Athenaise
MINE DE RIEN / Christian Barani / Guillaume Reynard / Auto Production
À L'EST DU PARADIS / Lech Kowalski / Agat Films & Compagnie
CLARA B / Corinne Ibram / Alexandru Solomon / Seppia
TROPICO DE CANCER (TROPIQUE DU CANCER) / Eugenio Polgovsky / Centro de Capacitacion
LOULOU ET GÉGÉ / Marianne Gosset / Les Films d'ici
FANDANGO / Sandhya Suri
L'HOMME INDIEN (L' ROI INDIA - SAFAR - OLE REIS) / Maciej Drygas / ADR Productions

15.

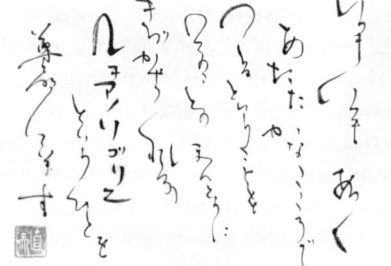

16.

17.

18.

19.

20.

21.

16. "Constantly, / and tirelessly, / with a warm hearth / he welcomes / the act of creation. / To Luciano Rigolini/ I give all my respect / and gratitude." Naomi Kawase's tribute to L.R., 2006
17. L.R. with Tsai Ming-liang at the film premiere of *Journey to the West*, Paris, 2014
18. L.R. with the filmmaker Lech Kowalsky and producers at the Venice Film Festival 2005, winner of the Orizzonti Award for Best Documentary with the film *East of Paradise*
19. L.R. with the filmmaker Alain Cavalier, Paris, 2022
20. L.R. with the filmmaker Apichatpong Weerasethakul at the Cannes Film Festival for the film premiere of *Mekong Hotel*, 2012
21. The Jury of the Swiss Film Award 2003. Luciano Rigolini in the centre with the filmmaker Daniel Schmid

All photos: Luciano Rigolini archive

22. *What You See*, solo exhibition at the Fotostiftung Schweiz, Winterthur 2008, exhibition poster and artist's book, Lars Müller Publishers, Baden, 2008, cover. Photo: Luciano Rigolini archive

LR: Sì, la rinuncia allo scatto riflette in parte quello che ho indicato nella risposta precedente. Mi pare utile citare a questo proposito un passaggio del manifesto del movimento neo-appropriazionista presentato nel 2011 ad Arles nell'ambito dei *Rencontres de la photographie*: «Adesso, siamo una specie di editori, noi tutti ricicliamo, tagliamo e incolliamo, scarichiamo e remixiamo. Possiamo far fare tutto alle immagini. Tutto ciò di cui abbiamo bisogno è un occhio, un cervello, una macchina fotografica, un telefono, un computer, uno scanner, un punto di vista [...]. Noi creiamo più che mai, perché le nostre risorse sono illimitate e le possibilità infinite [...]. Questo potenziale tecnologico ha delle ripercussioni estetiche. Cambia il concetto stesso di creazione. [...] Vogliamo ridare a questi lavori un nuovo statuto». Queste riflessioni in merito alla situazione attuale dell'immagine sono indubbiamente pertinenti, per me l'atto concettuale costituisce un atto di creazione. Un punto veramente centrale del mio lavoro risiede nella rilettura, attraverso un atto di appropriazione, di immagini anonime e di documenti senza alcun valore artistico, per conferire loro un nuovo statuto.

MF: La tua prima opera creata con immagini realizzate da anonimi è stata *What you see*, com'è nata?

LR: *What you see* (2008) è stato il mio primo libro d'autore e una delle mie prime mostre, alla Fotostiftung a Winterthur, in termini di appropriazione. Si tratta di foto intime amatoriali, non riuscite, sbagliate, ma non solo. Il lavoro di selezione delle immagini è durato una decina di anni. Le ho rilette e accostate in un libro, in modo da creare un discorso estetico-narrativo personale che le portasse su un altro piano. Ho voluto così sfatare l'atto creativo dell'artista, perché si tratta di fotografie anonime, delle quali mi sono semplicemente appropriato attraverso la mia sensibilità. È in questa dinamica fra immagine trovata e lettura personale che risiede la tensione creativa del mio approccio alla fotografia.

MF: È evidente nel tuo lavoro il ricorrere di immagini provenienti dall'industria meccanica e da quella automobilistica. Ci potresti raccontare le ragioni di questa evidente fascinazione?

LR: Le ragioni sono personali, hanno a che vedere con la mia iniziale formazione di disegnatore di macchine e con la mia fascinazione, da sempre, per la meccanica e per le macchine. Non posso non citare a questo proposito *Le macchine celibi* (1975) di Jean Clair e Harald Szeemann. Riguardo all'altro aspetto del mio lavoro, cioè la mia attrazione per l'industria automobilistica degli anni Cinquanta e Sessanta, vi sono due serie di lavori paradigmatici di questa mia propensione, *Surrogates* e *Mask*.

«Un punto veramente centrale del mio lavoro risiede nella rilettura, attraverso un atto di appropriazione, di immagini anonime e di documenti senza alcun valore artistico, per conferire loro un nuovo statuto».

23. *Mask*, artist's book, Edition Patrick Frey, Zurich, 2015, cover

Il primo, presentato in una mostra dal titolo *Concept Car* al Musée de l'Elysée di Losanna (2012) e al Centre culturel suisse a Parigi (2012), era composto da una serie di immagini – trovate su un sito d'asta in Internet – di pezzi di ricambio di automobili d'occasione, selezionate e riprodotte da parte mia senza manipolazione né della messa in pagina né dei colori. Per la realizzazione di *Surrogates* (2012) il lavoro di selezione è stato lungo e minuzioso, ho dovuto scegliere tra migliaia di immagini. Nella sequenza realizzata per le mostre e per il libro omonimo, mi sono lasciato guidare dai rimandi all'estetica dei movimenti della storia dell'arte del Novecento, che sorprendentemente affiorano anche in queste immagini che all'origine non avevano alcun intento artistico o estetico. Il libro *Mask* (2015) presenta una serie di frontali di automobili americane realizzate fra il 1955 e il 1962, periodo durante il quale lo sviluppo dell'ingegneria tecnologica ha permesso delle possibilità creative inedite all'industria automobilistica. Ad interessarmi è stata la potente dimensione scultorea dei paraurti e dei frontali, che ritagliati in modo da eliminare qualsiasi contestualizzazione esaltano le forme rendendole di volta in volta insolite e surreali. Anche in questo caso ho attinto ad un catalogo privo di qualsiasi intento estetico, realizzato come manuale per i carrozzieri per il montaggio delle griglie frontali. Ho ripreso le immagini e le ho riprodotte senza interventi grafici o fotografici, ma la sequenza elaborata per il libro ha conferito uno statuto radicalmente nuovo alle immagini, che hanno trovato così una loro legittima collocazione nell'estetica contemporanea.

MF: Per molti fotografi l'avvento del digitale ha comportato una rimessa in discussione del mezzo,

sense, it may be helpful to quote a passage from the manifesto of the neo-appropriationist movement presented at the Rencontres d'Arles in 2011: "Now, we're a series of editors. We all recycle, clip and cut, remix and upload. We can make images do anything. All we need is an eye, a brain, a camera, a phone, a computer, a scanner, a point of view … We create more than ever before, because our resources are unlimited and the possibilities endless … This technological potential has aesthetic repercussions. It changes the very concept of creation … We want to give these works

"A key feature of my work lies in the reworking, via an act of appropriation, of anonymous images and documents with no artistic value, to give them a new status."

a new status." These reflections on the current state of the image are undoubtedly pertinent; for me, the conceptual act is an act of creation. A key feature of my work lies in the reworking, via an act of appropriation, of anonymous images and documents with no artistic value, to give them a new status.

MF: Your first work made using images by anonymous photographers was *What you see*. How did it originate?

LR: *What you see* (2008) was my first book and one of my first exhibitions, at the Fotostiftung in Winterthur, on the subject of appropriation. They are intimate amateur photos, which are botched and full of faults, but that's not all. The job of selecting the images took about ten years. I reworked and juxtaposed them in a book to create a personal narrative-aesthetic viewpoint that would take them to another level. I thus wanted to debunk the creative act of the artist, because these are anonymous photographs, which I have simply appropriated using my sensitivity. It is in this dynamic between found image and personal interpretation that the creative tension of my approach to photography lies.

MF: The recurrent use of images from the mechanical and automotive industries is evident in your work, could you tell us the reasons for this obvious fascination?

LR: The reasons are personal; they have to do with my early training as a mechanical draughtsman and my lifelong fascination with machines and cars. In this respect, I should mention *The Bachelor Machines* (1975) by Jean Clair and Harald Szeemann. Regarding the other aspect of my work – my fascination with the automotive industry of the 1950s and 1960s – there are two series of works that are emblematic of this propensity: *Surrogates* and *Mask*.

The former, presented at the *Concept Car* exhibition at the Musée de l'Élysée in Lausanne (2012) and at the Centre culturel suisse in Paris (2012), was composed of a series of images of second-hand car parts, found on an internet auction site, which I selected and reproduced without manipulating either the layout or the colours. The selection process for *Surrogates* (2012) was long and painstaking, as I had to choose from thousands of images. In the sequence created for the exhibitions and the book of the same title, I was guided by the references to the aesthetics of the 20th-century art-historical movements that surprisingly also surface in these images originally devoid of artistic or aesthetic intentions. The book *Mask* (2015) presents a series of grilles from American cars made between 1955 and 1962, when the development of technological engineering allowed unprecedented creative possibilities for the automotive industry. What interested me was the powerful sculptural dimension of the bumpers and grilles that, cut out in such a way as to remove all context, emphasize the forms, making them unusual and surreal. Again, I drew on a catalogue without any aesthetic intentions, which was created as an assembly manual for body shops. I took the images and reproduced them without any graphic or photographic manipulation, but the sequence developed for the book gave them a radically new status, allowing them to find their legitimate place in contemporary aesthetics.

24. *Concept Car*, solo exhibition at Musée de l'Élysée, Lausanne, 2012, invitation card

25. *Surrogates*, artist's book, ed. Centre culturel suisse, Paris, Musée de l'Élysée, Lausanne, 2012, cover

MF: For many photographers, the advent of the digital age has meant rethinking the medium, but in your case it has opened up new avenues for experimenting and using new languages. Can you tell us about this?

LR: The experience of teaching at university and exchanging ideas with young people was certainly very stimulating. Teaching photography and film necessarily involves coming into contact with new creative modes and ideas, so I did not see the advent of digital photography and new technologies as an obstacle. On the contrary, technological innovations, commencing precisely with the discovery of photography, have always offered new development opportunities for art history and aesthetics. Moreover, I consider the presence of quotations in many of my works, for example *Surrogates*, a meaningful continuity of dialogue with art history.

MF: It is above all in your art books that the relationship with art history is most evident. How are they born, how do you proceed from conception to creation?

LR: First of all, I would like to stress that my publications almost always have a direct, thematic

nel tuo caso però ha aperto nuove vie per sperimentare e utilizzare linguaggi inediti. Puoi parlarci di questo aspetto?

LR: Sicuramente mi ha molto stimolato l'esperienza dell'insegnamento universitario e dello scambio con i giovani. L'insegnamento in ambito fotografico e cinematografico comporta la necessità di entrare in contatto con nuove modalità creative e idee, di conseguenza non ho mai considerato l'avvento del digitale e di nuove tecnologie come un ostacolo. Al contrario, le innovazioni tecnologiche hanno sempre offerto, a partire proprio dalla scoperta della fotografia, nuove opportunità di sviluppo per la storia dell'arte e per l'estetica. Peraltro, la dimensione citazionista presente in molti miei lavori, ad esempio in *Surrogates*, la considero una pregnante continuità di discorso rispetto alla storia dell'arte.

MF: È soprattutto nei tuoi libri d'autore che si può evincere con maggiore evidenza il rapporto con la storia dell'arte. Come nascono, come procedi dall'ideazione alla realizzazione?

LR: Innanzitutto ci tengo a sottolineare che le mie pubblicazioni sono quasi sempre in relazione diretta, tematica e formale, con le opere fotografiche, ma al contempo i libri costituiscono delle vere e proprie opere autonome. Per quanto riguarda la progettazione e la realizzazione, ho il privilegio di poter contare sulla collaborazione attiva di Sidi Vanetti, artista e grafico estrema-

« A me interessava la possibilità di trasformare delle fotografie scientifiche documentarie in opere evocative della dimensione mitologica e sognante che da sempre accompagna l'uomo che guarda la luna ».

mente creativo, con il quale abbiamo sviluppato una complicità e una sintonia straordinarie. È attraverso questa collaborazione che si precisano le mie idee e le mie visioni.

MF: L'oggettività e la dimensione freddamente concettuale del tuo lavoro non escludono una dimensione mitica e poetica, anche quando il cuore della questione è quello della verità o della plausibilità della fotografia. Mi riferisco, evidentemente, alle opere realizzate a partire dagli archivi della NASA e a quelle sugli UFO.

LR: In effetti, il libro *AS 15-16* pubblicato da Patrick Frey contiene immagini scattate dagli astronauti delle missioni lunari Apollo 15 e Apollo 16. Ancora una volta, fotografie scattate per scopi scientifici, ma che nella sequenza narrativa del volume e nell'approccio concettuale all'immagine acquisiscono una dimensione estetica che rimanda alla *land art* e all'arte minimalista. L'ordinamento delle immagini nel libro offre una sorta di viaggio metaforico sulla luna. A me interessava la possibilità di trasformare delle fotografie scientifiche documentarie in opere evocative della dimensione mitologica e sognante che da sempre accompagna l'uomo che guarda la luna.

Sempre guardando al cielo, ho realizzato nel 2022 *Inexplicata Volantes*, pubblicato dall'editore giapponese Akio Nagasawa. Le immagini vintage contenute nel libro le ho recuperate da un centro ufologico e le ho riprodotte senza alcuna manipolazione. Il loro utilizzo trascende il soggetto a favore della dimensione estetica. Ogni graffio, segno, polvere, unitamente alle diverse tonalità cromatiche, accentua la natura pittorica delle immagini. Tra l'altro, l'unico testo presente nel libro è un passaggio della Bibbia che fa riferimento a questo tipo di visioni. *Inexplicata Volantes* è l'espressione della mia irrinunciabile necessità di indagare il potere poetico delle immagini.

MF: Negli sviluppi più recenti della tua ricerca irrompe, e non sorprende, anche l'intelligenza artificiale.

LR: La fotografia, nella sua evoluzione, è sempre stata legata alla tecnologia. Per quanto riguarda l'immagine generata attraverso l'intelligenza artificiale, è unicamente questa fase tecnologica iniziale non ancora codificata a interessarmi. È nella dimensione «pionieristica» attuale che tutte le possibilità sono aperte per interrogare l'immagine, la sua verità e la sua natura, con modalità finora sconosciute. Come sempre il mio approccio è concettuale, mentre non ho alcun interesse per l'imitazione del reale o per il realismo. A motivarmi è esclusivamente la potenzialità di generare opere dove l'ambiguità fra la qualità pittorica e quella fotografica tende a rendere difficoltosa l'identificazione dell'immagine. In un certo senso, in questi lavori recenti sull'architettura realizzati con l'AI riconosco un sottile *fil rouge* con l'estetica delle mie prime fotografie sulle città, soprattutto nei rimandi alle composizioni astratte delle avanguardie.

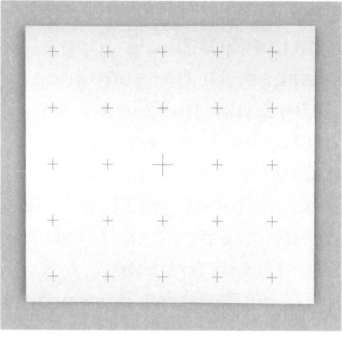

26. Luciano Rigolini with Sidi Vanetti, graphic designer, 2017. *AS 15-16*, artist's book, 2018, cover. Photo: Luciano Rigolini archive

and formal relationship with the photographic works, but at the same time the books are true autonomous works. In terms of design and realisation, I am privileged to be able to count on the active collaboration of Sidi Vanetti, an extremely creative artist and graphic designer, with

"I was interested in the possibility of transforming documentary scientific photographs into works evoking the mythological and dreamlike dimension that has always accompanied humans looking at the moon."

whom I have established an extraordinary complicit and attuned relationship. It is through this partnership that my ideas and visions are refined.

MF: The objectivity and the cool conceptual dimension of your work do not preclude a mythical and poetic dimension, even when the crux of the issue is the truth or plausibility of the photograph. I'm referring, of course, to the works based on images from the NASA and UFO archives.

LR: Indeed, the book *AS 15-16*, published by Patrick Frey, features images taken by the astronauts of the Apollo 15 and Apollo 16 lunar missions. Once again, they are photographs taken for scientific purposes, but which, in the narrative sequence of the book and the conceptual approach to the image, acquire an aesthetic dimension that recalls Land art and Minimalist art. The order of the images in the book offers a kind of metaphorical journey to the moon. I was interested in the possibility of transforming documentary scientific photographs into works evoking the mythological and dreamlike dimension that has always accompanied humans looking at the moon.

Still looking at the sky, I produced *Inexplicata Volantes* in 2022, released by Japanese publisher Akio Nagasawa. I retrieved the vintage images in the book from a ufology centre and reproduced them without any manipulation. Their use transcends the subject in favour of the aesthetic dimension. The pictorial nature of the images is accentuated by each scratch, mark and speck of dust, along with the different colour tones. By the way, the only text in the book is a passage from the Bible that refers to this type of vision. *Inexplicata Volantes* is an expression of my inescapable need to explore the poetic power of images.

MF: Not surprisingly, artificial intelligence has also entered the picture in the latest developments in your work.

LR: Throughout its evolution, photography has always been linked to technology. As far as AI-generated images are concerned, it is only this initial technological phase that has yet to be codified that interests me. It is in the current "pioneering" dimension that all possibilities are open to probe the image, its truth and its nature, in hitherto unknown ways. As always, my approach is conceptual, while I have no interest in imitating reality or in realism. What motivates me is solely the potential to generate works where ambiguity between the pictorial and the photographic tends to make it difficult to identify the image. In a way, I recognise a subtle common thread with the aesthetics of my early photographs of cities in these recent works on architecture made using artificial intelligence, especially in the references to the abstract compositions of the avant-gardes.

27. Luciano Rigolini with Akio Nagasawa launching *Inexplicata Volantes*, artist's book, Akio Nagasawa Publishing, Tokyo (JP), at Paris Photo, 2022. Photo: Luciano Rigolini archive

28. Luciano Rigolini with the students at the Documentary Master of the Pompeu Fabra University in Barcelona, 2019. Photo: Luciano Rigolini archive

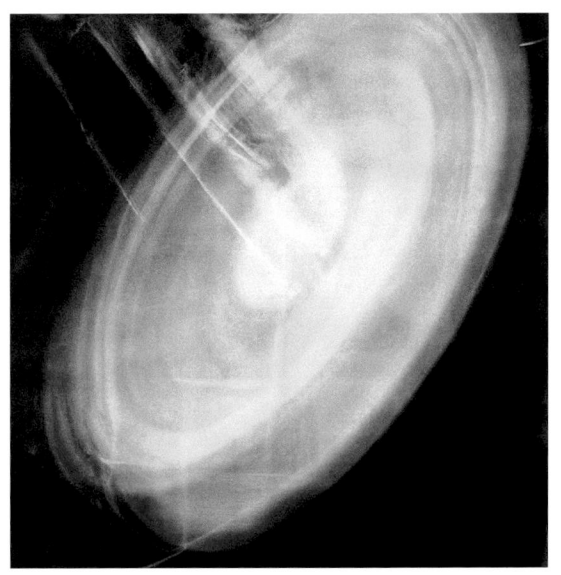

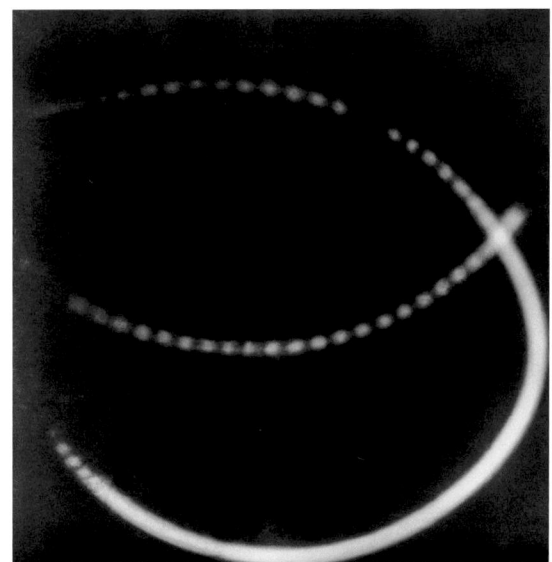

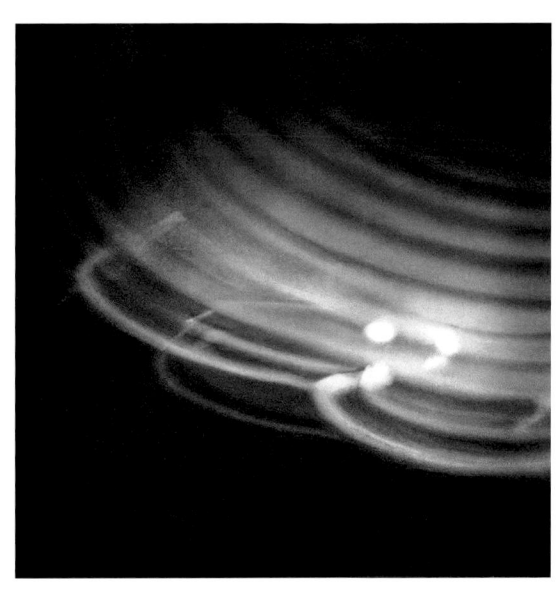

G

H

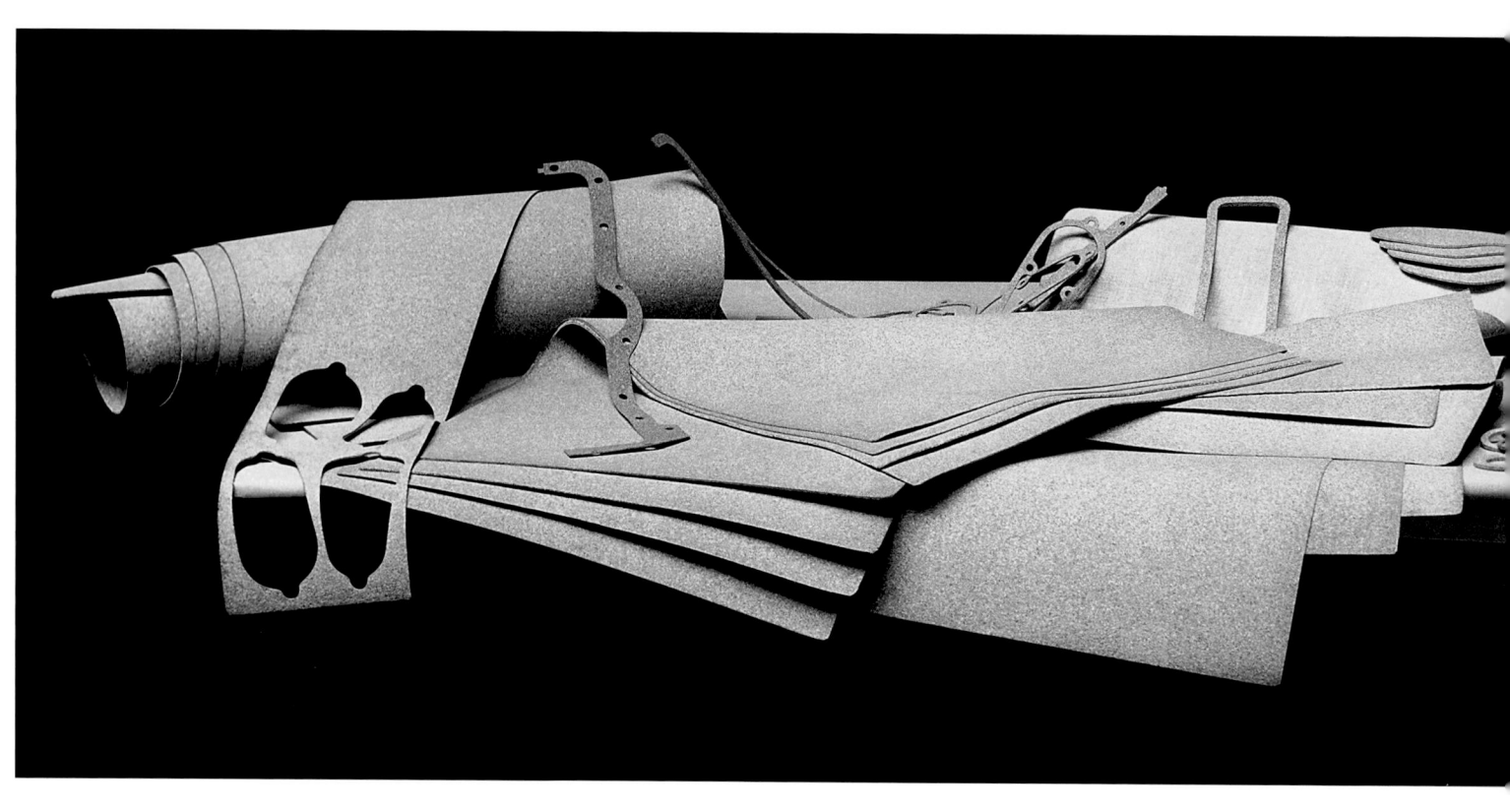

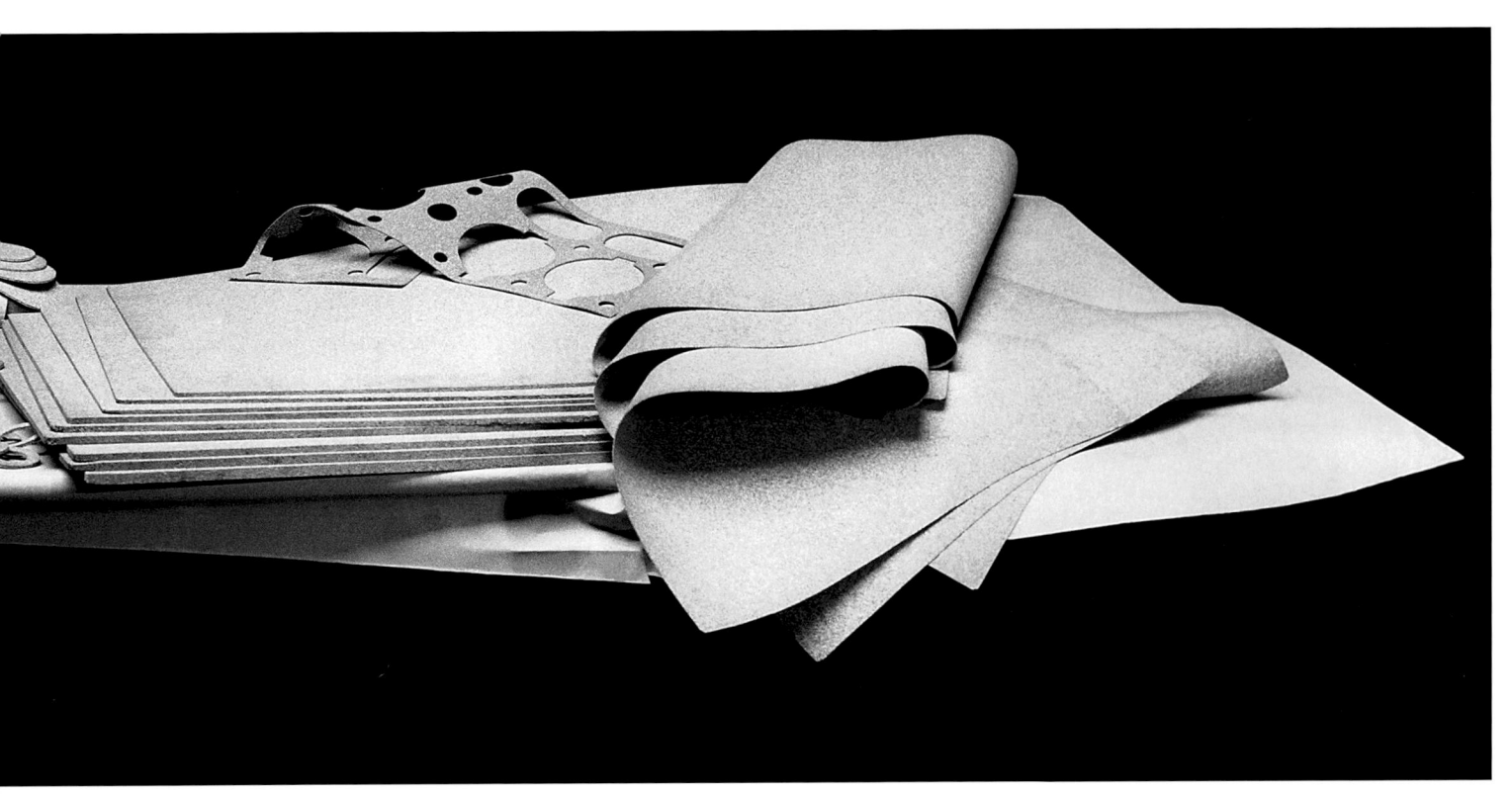

Luciano Rigolini

Interrogare l'immagine

di Marco Franciolli

L'attività artistica di Luciano Rigolini è multiforme e comprende la fotografia, la realizzazione di libri d'artista e la produzione di film documentari d'autore. Un *fil rouge* unisce le diverse modalità espressive, che si intrecciano e si arricchiscono reciprocamente in un originale percorso ontologico volto ad indagare lo statuto dell'immagine contemporanea e ad approfondire il rapporto che l'immagine intrattiene con il reale. La rilevanza della sua intensa attività artistica, ormai estesa su oltre trent'anni, è attestata da numerosi premi e riconoscimenti a livello nazionale e internazionale in ambito fotografico e cinematografico.

Gli esordi fotografici di Rigolini hanno inizio nel 1990 con un ciclo dal titolo *Paesaggi urbani*, immagini in bianco e nero di grande formato che ritraggono lo spazio urbano attraverso un peculiare punto di vista che tende a scardinare la visione prospettica tradizionale a favore di una composizione geometrizzante che richiama gli stilemi del collage costruttivista. Il taglio compositivo in queste immagini è frutto unicamente della scelta del punto di vista, senza alcuna manipolazione del negativo o in fase di stampa. La serie dei *Paesaggi urbani* si protrae fino al 2002, ma in parallelo Rigolini intraprende un percorso creativo che lo porta a rinunciare progressivamente all'atto fisico della ripresa a favore del recupero di immagini fotografiche di anonimi. L'artista attinge così a un fondo iconografico inesauribile, appropriandosi di immagini realizzate da altri con intenti e scopi vari per rielaborarle secondo un proprio programma estetico e concettuale fino a trasformarle in opere proprie. Punto d'avvio per questo nuovo indirizzo creativo è una raccolta di fotografie collezionate da Rigolini nel corso di dieci anni e assemblate per costituire una propria opera dal titolo *What you see*, presentata in una mostra presso la Fotostiftung Schweiz per la Fotografia a Winterthur nel 2008. Con lo stesso titolo, l'artista realizza anche un libro, primo di una serie di volumi che costituiscono in realtà delle vere e proprie opere autonome. Infatti, parallelamente alla produzione di cicli fotografici, Rigolini realizza con regolarità libri d'artista che ribadiscono il carattere fortemente concettuale sotteso a tutta la sua produzione artistica; la scelta delle immagini, la sequenza e la composizione grafica determinano una narrazione inedita e autonoma, che trascende la valenza iconica originaria. La pulsione compulsiva a ricercare e collezionare immagini fotografiche da archivi oppure nel web manifesta un elemento fondante del suo discorso estetico: l'ossessione per l'immagine. Ad attrarre l'attenzione dell'artista sono soprattutto immagini fotografiche provenienti da archivi dell'industria meccanica e automobilistica.

La ventennale esperienza di Luciano Rigolini – a partire dal 1995 – quale produttore di film documentari d'autore per ARTE, la rete televisiva culturale franco-tedesca con sede a Parigi, ha indubbiamente contribuito ad ampliare e arricchire ulteriormente la sua ricerca personale sullo statuto dell'immagine. La trasmissione *La Lucarne*, della quale è stato ideatore e responsabile, ha offerto uno spazio di straordinaria libertà per il cinema d'autore, sperimentale e indipendente. L'ideale che ha guidato le scelte di Luciano Rigolini nel corso degli anni presso ARTE è stato quello di portare l'arte dentro il mezzo televisivo ed è con tale intento che ha sviluppato proficue collaborazioni con artisti e registi fra i più marcanti e originali della scena cinematografica internazionale. È nell'ambito dell'attività dedicata al documentario che Luciano Rigolini ha avuto anche l'opportunità di confrontarsi con le questioni di fondo del rapporto di ambiguità che l'immagine intrattiene con la realtà e un evidente riverbero di tali riflessioni lo si può cogliere nell'evoluzione della produzione di opere fotografiche e nei libri. Esemplare in tal senso il ciclo dedicato alle fotografie della luna riprese dall'archivio della NASA relative alle missioni Apollo 15 e Apollo 16. Rigolini integra in modo inedito la passione per la storia dell'arte e della fotografia con le tecniche di stampa digitale per creare, a partire da fotografie scientifiche prive di qualsiasi intento estetico, immagini nuove, opere ambigue in bilico fra natura pittorica e fotografica. L'artista concentra la propria attenzione sulla proprietà dell'immagine fotografica di attivare percorsi di lettura insoliti e in tal senso non sorprende l'interesse per le fotografie di UFO, oggetti volanti la cui immagine è resa plausibile unicamente dal dubbio. Le stampe di fotografie analogiche, attinte da un archivio di ufologia, vengono trasposte dall'artista su supporto digitale e stampate in un grande formato che modifica la natura stessa dell'immagine e produce una *mise en abyme* del soggetto, ripreso nel volume *Inexplicata Volantes*, pubblicato nel 2022 dall'editore giapponese Akio Nagasawa.

La fase più recente di Rigolini vede l'avvio di un nuovo percorso creativo con immagini generate utilizzando gli algoritmi dell'intelligenza artificiale. Dopo aver rinunciato allo scatto fotografico, Rigolini

si astiene ora dall'utilizzare immagini fotografiche scattate da anonimi a favore di icone prodotte a partire da indicazioni molto dettagliate fornite dall'artista all'intelligenza artificiale. Il confine sempre più labile fra la natura fotografica e quella pittorica nelle opere di Luciano Rigolini viene ulteriormente stemperato in un ciclo di immagini che sembrano riprese fotografiche di architetture industriali dismesse. In realtà attraverso l'elaborazione virtuale di forme, colori e strutture, l'artista afferma in modo inequivocabile che l'immagine fotografica è sempre e soltanto un simulacro della realtà.

Dal 1989 Marco Franciolli ha curato mostre e pubblicazioni dedicate a temi di arte moderna e contemporanea, fotografia e architettura. È stato direttore-conservatore del Museo Cantonale d'arte e primo direttore del Museo d'arte della Svizzera italiana MASI a Lugano. Dal 2018 svolge attività di curatore e critico d'arte indipendente.

Luciano Rigolini

Probing the image

by Marco Franciolli

Luciano Rigolini's work as an artist is highly diverse, encompassing photography, the creation of artist's books and the production of auteur documentary films. The various modes of expression are joined by a common thread, intertwining and mutually enriching each other on an original metaphysical journey aimed at investigating the status of the contemporary image and exploring the relationship between image and reality. The significance of his intense artistic career, now spanning more than 30 years, is attested by numerous national and international awards and prizes in the fields of photography and film.

Rigolini made his debut as a photographer in 1990 with a cycle entitled *Paesaggi urbani* (urban landscapes): large-format black-and-white pictures portraying urban space from unusual viewpoints that tend to disrupt the traditional perspectival view in favour of a geometrical composition recalling the stylistic features of constructivist collage. In these images, the composition is derived solely from the choice of viewpoint, without any manipulation of the negative or during the printing stage. The *Paesaggi urbani* series continued until 2002, but during the same time Rigolini embarked on a creative path that led him to gradually give up the physical act of taking photographs, preferring instead to retrieve images by anonymous photographers. This allowed him to draw on an inexhaustible iconographic reservoir, appropriating images made by others with various intentions and purposes in order to rework them according to his own aesthetic and conceptual agenda, transforming them into his own works. The starting point for this new creative direction was a collection of photographs collected by Rigolini over a ten-year period and assembled to form his own work entitled *What You See*, presented at an exhibition at the Fotostiftung Schweiz in Winterthur in 2008. He also produced a book with the same title, the first in a series of what are actually stand-alone works. Indeed, alongside his photographic cycles, Rigolini regularly produces artist's books that confirm the strongly conceptual nature of his entire artistic output; the choice of images, sequence and graphic composition establish an unprecedented and autonomous narrative that transcends the original figurative value. The compulsive urge to search for and collect photographs from archives or online reveals a key feature of his aesthetic language: an obsession with images. His attention was caught in particular by photographs from archives of the mechanical and automotive industry.

Rigolini's 20 years of experience – commencing in 1995 – as a producer of auteur documentary films for ARTE, the Paris-based Franco-German cultural television channel, undoubtedly contributed to broadening and further enriching his personal exploration of the status of the image. The *La Lucarne* programme, which he created and managed, offered a space that provided extraordinary freedom for auteur, experimental and independent films. The ideal that guided Rigolini's choices over his years at ARTE was to bring art into the medium of television, and it was with this intention that he established fruitful partnerships with some of the most influential and original artists and directors on the international film scene. In the sphere of his documentary work Rigolini has also had the opportunity to engage with the fundamental questions relating to

the ambiguous relationship that the image has with reality, and a clear reflection of these observations can be glimpsed in the evolution of his photographic production and in his books. A good example is the series dedicated to photographs of the moon taken from the NASA archive of the Apollo 15 and Apollo 16 missions. Rigolini innovatively combines his passion for history of art and photography with digital printing techniques, creating new images from scientific photographs without any artistic intentions, ambiguous works poised between the pictorial and the photographic. The artist focuses his attention on the photographic image's property of activating unusual reading paths, and in this sense it comes as no surprise to learn of his interest in photographs of UFOs, flying objects whose image is made plausible solely by doubt. He transposes prints of analogue photographs, taken from a ufology archive, onto a digital medium before printing them in a large format that alters the very nature of the image, creating a *mise en abyme* of the subject, portrayed in the book *Inexplicata Volantes*, released in 2022 by the Japanese publisher Akio Nagasawa.

Rigolini's most recent phase marks the beginning of a new creative journey with images generated using AI algorithms. After having given up taking photographs, Rigolini now also avoids using photographic images taken by anonymous people in favour of icons produced from very detailed instructions that the artist gives to artificial intelligence. The increasingly blurred boundary between the photographic and the pictorial in Rigolini's works becomes even hazier in a series of images resembling photographs of abandoned industrial architecture. In reality, the virtual processing of shapes, colours and structures enables the artist to unequivocally state that the photographic image is only ever a simulacrum of reality.

Marco Franciolli has been curating exhibitions and publications on modern and contemporary art, photography and architecture since 1989. He was director-conservator of the Museo Cantonale d'Arte and first director of MASI (Museo d'arte della Svizzera italiana) LAC in Lugano. Since 2018, he has worked as an independent curator and art critic.

[DE → p. 9, FR → p. 10]

Biography

Born in Tesserete, Ticino, 2 August 1950.
Lives and works in Lugano and Paris.

Studied Cinema at Paris VIII University.

Achieved international acclaim in the 1990s with *Urban Landscapes*, a photographic work through which he explores the specificity of the medium and the aesthetic relationships between photography and painting.

1995–2015 Worked for the European cultural TV channel ARTE in Paris, where he was responsible for creative auteur film development.
While continuing his photographic work and research into new forms of narration and language, he produced films by filmmakers such as Chris Marker, Alexandre Sokourov, Naomi Kawase, Chantal Akerman, Apichatpong Weerasethakul, Tsai Ming-liang, Wang Bing and Laurie Anderson.

Since 2002 Has been working in photography exclusively through appropriation and rereading of amateur images and industrial documents. His work is also expressed through several artist's books.

1997–2022 Jury member or commissioner of various national and international film festivals (Festival international du cinéma documentaire Visions du Réel, Nyon; Mumbai International Film Festival Miff; Taiwan International Documentary Festival, Taipei; Rencontres Internationales de la Photographie d'Arles; International Documentary Film Festival Amsterdam-IDFA; Yamagata International Documentary Film Festival; Festival del Film Locarno; Nara International Film festival, Nara; Internationale Kurzfilmtage Winterthur; DOK Leipzig; Sarajevo Film Festival; doclisboa, Lisbon).

Since 1994 Has taught Cinema and Photography at several universities, including RICE University in Houston, SCI-Arc (Southern California Institute of Architecture), HEAD (Geneva School of Art and Design), and the Creative Documentary Master at POMPEU FABRA University in Barcelona.

Exhibitions (selection)
*solo exhibitions

1987 *Luciano Rigolini: film sur l'art, Cinéma du Musée*, Musée nationale d'art moderne, Centre Georges Pompidou, Paris (FR)
1992 *Luciano Rigolini. Fotografie '90–'92*, Museo Cantonale d'Arte, Lugano
1995 *Luciano Rigolin: Città Aperta–Open City. Photographs 1990-1995*, Farish Gallery, RICE University School of Architecture, Houston (US).
Contemporary Photography from the Gernsheim Collection, Roemer und Pelizaeus Museum, Hildesheim (DE)
1997 *Zürich – Ein Fotoportrait*, Kunsthaus Zürich, Zurich.
Icons: Magnets of Meaning, San Francisco Museum of Modern Art, San Francisco (US).
Architecture in Black and White, Kunst- und Ausstellungshalle der BRD, Bonn (DE)
1998 *Digital Image Manipulation*, CACT Centro d'Arte Contemporanea Ticino, Bellinzona
1999 *Opere del XX. secolo dalla collezione permanente*, Museo Cantonale d'Arte, Lugano
2001 *PARIS PHOTO*, Carrousel du Louvre, Galerie Renn 14/16 Verneuil, Paris (FR)
2005–08 *PhotoSuisse*, Centro Culturale Svizzero, Rome (IT); Centre PasquArt, Biel; Pinacoteca Casa Rusca, Locarno; Bunkier Sztuki Contemporary Art Gallery, Krakow (PL); Centro de la Imagen, Mexico City (MX); Museo de arte Zapopan, Jalisco (MX)
2007 **Luciano Rigolini. La forma dello sguardo. Fotografie 1990–2007*, Museo Cantonale d'Arte, Lugano
2008 **What You See*, Fotostiftung Schweiz, Winterthur
2011 *Schweizer Fotobücher des 20. Jahrhunderts. Eine andere Fotogeschichte*, Fotostiftung Schweiz, Winterthur.
**Luciano Rigolini. Un' altra immagine*, m.a.x. museo – Spazio Officina, Chiasso
2012 **Surrogates*, Centre culturel suisse, Paris (FR).
**Concept Car*, Musée de l'Élysée, Lausanne
2015 **Landscape*, Buchmann Art Galerie, Lugano
2017 *Auto/Photo*, Fondation Cartier pour l'art contemporain, Paris (FR).
Fotografia Europea – European Photography, Reggio Emilia (IT)

2018 *Pendulum. Moving goods, moving people*, Fondazione Mast, Bologna (IT).
Noi e il MASI. Donazione Giancarlo e Danna Olgiati, Museo d'arte della Svizzera italiana – MASI, Lugano

2019 *Moonstruck: Photographic Explorations*, Fotostiftung Schweiz, Winterthur

2024 **FOTOGRAFIA*, Fondazione d'Arte Erich Lindenberg, Porza

Publications (selection)

1992 *Luciano Rigolini. Fotografie '90–'92*, Museo Cantonale d'Arte, Lugano (catalogue)

1993 *Luciano Rigolini photographs 1990–1995 / Città aperta. Open City*, Rice University, Houston (US) (portfolio)

1996 *European Photography. Art Magazine*, no. 59, ed. Andreas Müller-Pohle, Göttingen (DE) (portfolio).
Spot, Deconstructing the City, ed. Houston Center of Photography (US) (portfolio)

1997 *Zürich*, ed. Guido Magnaguagno, Giorgio von Arb, Offizin Verlag, Zurich (catalogue).
Icons: Magnets of Meaning, San Francisco Museum of Modern Art and Chronicle Books, San Francisco (US) (catalogue)

2000 *La photographie traversée, Cinéma-documentaire. Un réenchantement du monde*, by Luciano Rigolini and Christian Milovanoff, Rencontres internationales de la photographie – Arles, Actes Sud, Arles (FR) (catalogue)

2001 *Topos, Von Verschwinden der Stadt. Deconstructing the City*, European Landscape Magazine, n. 34, Munich (DE) (portfolio).
Une Tour, ed. Textuel, Paris (FR)

2002 *L'architecture d'aujourd'hui*, n. 341, ed. Jean Michel Place, Paris (FR) (portfolio)

2004 *PHOTOsuisse. Luciano Rigolini*, DVD and book, ed. Televisione Svizzera SRG SSR idée suisse and Lars Müller Publishers, Baden.
Ritmo 04–Luciano Rigolini, artist's book published by the Museo Cantonale d'Arte, Lugano (winner, AIGA 50 Books/50 Covers competition 2005)

2007 *Luciano Rigolini. La forma dello sguardo, fotografie 1990–2007*, Mendrisio Academy Press, Mendrisio (exh. cat. Museo Cantonale d'Arte di Lugano)

2008 *What You See*, artist's book, ed. Lars Müller Publishers, Baden

2011 *Livres de photographie suisse de 1927 à nos jours. Une autre histoire de la photographie*, ed. Lars Müller Publishers, Baden and Fotostiftung Schweiz, Winterthur.
Luciano Rigolini. Un'altra immagine, Skira editore, Milan (IT) (exh. cat. Spazio Officina, Chiasso)

2012 *Surrogates*, artist's book, ed. Centre culturel suisse, Paris (FR), Musée de l'Élysée, Lausanne

2013 *Private / Used*, artist's book, Edition Patrick Frey, Zurich

2015 *Mask*, artist's book, Edition Patrick Frey, Zurich

2018 *AS 15-16*, artist's book, Edition Patrick Frey, Zurich

2022 *Inexplicata Volantes*, artist's book, Akio Nagasawa Publishing, Tokyo (JP)

2024 *Apparere*, artist's book, Editions Atelier EXB, Paris (FR)

Gran Premio svizzero di design 2024

Il Gran Premio svizzero di design omaggia carriere esemplari e offre visibilità a designer il cui lavoro apre prospettive o riflessioni particolarmente interessanti in questo campo.

Quali voci far sentire in un mondo così rumoroso come il nostro? Bisogna valorizzare coloro che generano idee per rendere più belli i nostri oggetti, i nostri manifesti, i nostri siti Internet e i nostri vestiti? Oppure coloro che li rendono più sostenibili? O forse va premiato chi vede nel design un atto sociale? Questa disciplina può essere portatrice di nuovi messaggi? Cosa significa, nel 2024, pensare e creare tenendo conto della diversità e della complessità del nostro mondo?

La giuria discute intensamente di questi temi e valuta con la massima attenzione il messaggio che intende trasmettere con l'attribuzione dei tre premi. Il suo intento è sempre quello di mettere in evidenza il lavoro di singoli individui che si distinguono per il loro approccio innovativo, creativo o impegnato oppure hanno influenzato o influenzano ancora in modo significativo la loro disciplina. E questo senza dimenticare le donne, che in passato hanno ricevuto poca visibilità. L'annuncio dei Gran Premi attira l'attenzione dei media e consente di far conoscere i diversi ambiti del design a un pubblico diversificato, ma non solo: il riconoscimento federale, conferito da pari, rende anche omaggio a professionisti e professioniste che esplorano i confini della propria pratica.

Nel 2024 sono state scelte persone che hanno intrapreso un percorso innovativo nel loro campo. Il contributo di Paola De Martin va ben oltre la ricerca tradizionale. Le sue riflessioni critiche guardano al design con un approccio transdisciplinare che si colloca in un determinato contesto sociale e politico e affronta questioni come la migrazione, il razzismo e l'esclusione sociale. La stilista Lucie Meier è protagonista di una carriera straordinaria: a soli 40 anni ha già lavorato per importanti case di moda come Louis Vuitton, Balenciaga, Dior et Jil Sander. Chi costruisce il proprio percorso professionale all'estero deve spesso attendere molto tempo prima che il suo operato venga riconosciuto in Svizzera. Il premio a Lucie Meier valorizza una designer che conosce nel profondo la propria disciplina. Infine, con i suoi 74 anni, Luciano Rigolini è un creatore che non ha mai smesso di interrogare le immagini. Esplora la sua materia facendola propria e si interessa in particolare alla fotografia vernacolare. Attraverso il suo sguardo, le fotografie rivelano nuove potenzialità plastiche. Tutto questo avviene in parallelo a una carriera internazionale comme produttore nel cinema documentario d'autore.

Riunendo sotto l'egida del Gran Premio svizzero di design 2024 tre personalità che si trovano in momenti diversi del loro percorso professionale e perseguono ognuna un approccio del tutto singolare, la giuria mostra che il

design apre molteplici prospettive. Riconoscere il lavoro di Paola De Martin, Lucie Meier e Luciano Rigolini, attivi in ambiti relativamente distanti fra loro, significa proprio questo. Le loro storie personali sono la prova che non è necessario appartenere a un'élite per aspirare al riconoscimento del proprio operato, perché gli elementi propulsori della loro creatività sono la riflessione e l'impegno.

Nathalie Herschdorfer, Presidente della Commissione federale del design

Prefazione

A 18 anni dal lancio, il Gran Premio svizzero di Design dell'Ufficio federale della cultura (UFC), il più alto riconoscimento per il design in Svizzera, continua a essere uno strumento eccezionale per mettere in luce le molteplici espressioni del design e la varietà degli sviluppi professionali in questo campo. Grazie alla valorizzazione di prospettive e approcci diversi, il nostro sguardo sull'importanza del design nella società diventa ogni anno più ricco e dinamico.

La prima edizione del Gran Premio svizzero di design si è tenuta nel 2007. Poco tempo prima l'UFC aveva abbandonato lo strumento dei contributi ai progetti di design e la Commissione federale del design (CFD) era alla ricerca di nuove possibilità per fornire a chi un sostegno finanziario mirato e proattivo alle eccellenze nel design.

Il primo anno, su proposta della CFD, sono stati assegnati cinque premi del valore di 40 000 franchi ciascuno. Due sono andati a personalità di fama internazionale: Adrian Frutiger, importante creatore di caratteri tipografici, e Bernhard Schobinger, uno dei più influenti designer di gioielli in Europa. Gli altri tre, invece, hanno voluto essere un riconoscimento alla generazione emergente e sono stati attribuiti all'agenzia Nose, fondata nel 1991, alla stilista Ruth Grüninger e al grafico Cornel Windlin, allora poco più che quarantenne. L'obiettivo dell'UFC era consentire a designer di talento di dedicarsi a progetti innovativi e sviluppare il loro potenziale creativo senza doversi concentrare esclusivamente sul successo commerciale.

I premi hanno segnato un pezzo di storia del design svizzero. La pubblicazione contiene spesso primi elementi d'archivio che poi serviranno come base per future presentazioni delle creazioni e per la ricerca. Proprio l'anno scorso si sono accesi i riflettore su diversi vincitori e vincitrici delle edizioni precedenti del Gran Premio svizzero di design: il Museo nazionale svizzero ha allestito una mostra monografica sull'eccezionale talento della stilista Ursula Rodel (premiata nel 2009); a settembre è stato pubblicato un catalogo completo dei lavori di Rosmarie Baltensweiler (premiata nel 2019), visionaria designer di lampade; Eleonore Peduzzi Riva (premiata nel 2023), l'architetta e designer che ha contribuito a sviluppare il celebre divano DS 600 e molto altro ancora, è stata più volte intervistata e invitata a partecipare a tavole rotonde; il Museum für Gestaltung di Zurigo ha esposto recentemente i magnifici tessuti di Claudia Caviezel (premiata nel 2016); Sarah Kueng e Lovis Caputo (premiate nel 2020) hanno ricevuto il meritato Goldene Hase della rivista Hochparterre, e la casa editrice About Books sta per pubblicare un volume con 12 nuovi tipi di carattere ideati da Rosmarie Tissi (premiata nel 2018).

Le vincitrici e il vincitore di quest'anno, Paola De Martin, Lucie Meier e Luciano Rigolini, hanno in comune la capacità di mettere in discussione le tradizioni e percorrere nuove strade. Con il loro approccio innovativo contribuiscono a promuovere la diversità, l'inclusione, l'etica, la collaborazione e la tecnologia nella cultura. Scoprite come tra le pagine di questa pubblicazione, che spero possa essere ricca di spunti interessanti e, come ogni anno, fonte di ispirazione per i vostri progetti futuri.

Anna Niederhäuser
Responsabile di design
Ufficio federale della cultura

Swiss Grand Award for Design 2024

The Swiss Grand Award for Design honours outstanding careers and casts a spotlight on creators whose work breaks new ground or explores interesting new intellectual avenues in this domain.

Which voices should we allow to be heard amidst the clamour of our world? Should we favour those whose creativity makes our objects, posters, websites or clothes more beautiful? What about those who make them more sustainable, or those who view design as a social practice? Can design convey new messages? What, in 2024, does it mean to think and create while acknowledging the diversity and complexity of our world?

The Jury engages in vigorous debate on these questions and pays a great deal of attention to the message it wishes to send out with its choice of three winners. It wants to showcase individuals with particularly innovative, creative or activist approaches as well as those that have influenced or continue to influence their discipline in a significant way – without forgetting women, of course, who were less visible in the past especially. The announcement of the Grand Award winners attracts media attention and gives the various design disciplines exposure to a broader public. An award sponsored by the federal government and handed out by peers is also a way of paying tribute to professionals who push the envelope in their chosen field and leave their mark on it through innovation, creativity or activism.

For 2024, we have chosen three innovators. Paola De Martin's work goes way beyond traditional research. She takes a critical view and a transdisciplinary approach to design, embedding it in a sociopolitical context by relating it to issues of migration, racism and social exclusion. The fashion designer Lucie Meier has had an enviable international career to date. Still only 40, she has worked for some of the great fashion houses, including Louis Vuitton, Balenciaga, Dior and Jil Sander. Recognition in Switzerland often comes late to those who pursue a career abroad, but Lucie Meier deserves this award due to her excellent, nuanced mastery of her craft. For his part, 74-year-old Luciano Rigolini has never tired of questioning images. He explores his material through appropriation, taking a particularly keen interest in vernacular photography and unlocking new dimensions of sculpturally. At the same time, he has pursued an international as a producer in auteur documentary films.

In selecting three individuals at different stages in their professional lives for the Swiss Grand Award for Design 2024, each with their own unique approach, the Jury highlights the variety of perspectives design can open up. The practices of Paola De Martin, Lucie Meier and Luciano Rigolini have relatively little in common and thus demonstrate the many career paths designers are free to choose. Their personal stories make it clear that

recognition does not hinge on being part of an elite: it can come through considered, committed creativity.

Nathalie Herschdorfer, Chair of the Federal Design Commission

Introduction

Even 18 years after the Swiss Grand Award for Design was launched, this highest honour for Swiss designers remains an outstanding instrument for the Federal Office of Culture (FOC) to showcase the wide range of potential career paths and the diversity of the design field. As we recognise a variety of different perspectives and approaches, our understanding of the importance of design for society as a whole is enriched and enlivened year by year.

The Grand Award was first presented in 2007. At that time, the FOC had recently discontinued its design project subsidies, and the Federal Design Commission was looking for new, more targeted and proactive ways to support designers with funding.

Five awards worth CHF 40,000 each were handed out in the first year at the Commission's suggestion. The winners included two internationally renowned personalities: the type designer Adrian Frutiger and Bernhard Schobinger, one of Europe's most influential jewellery artists. At the same time, the younger generation was represented by the design agency Nose, founded in 1991, as well as fashion designer Ruth Grüninger and graphic artist Cornel Windlin, who had only just turned 40. The FOC's aim was to enable design practitioners to work on innovative projects and develop their creative potential without having to focus solely on commercial success.

The Grand Award encapsulates a piece of Swiss design history. The accompanying publication often contains previously unseen archive pictures and serves as a basis for future work presentations and research projects. Just last year, a number of former winners were back in the spotlight. The Swiss National Museum hosted a monographic exhibition of the exceptionally talented Swiss fashion designer Ursula Rodel (Grand Award winner in 2009). An extensive catalogue of works by lighting design pioneer Rosmarie Baltensweiler (winner in 2019) was published in September. Eleonore Peduzzi Riva (winner in 2023), who had a hand in far more than just the world-famous DS-600 sofa, was invited to a number of panels and interviews. Zurich's Museum für Gestaltung presented the wonderful textile works of Claudia Caviezel (winner in 2016), while at the end of the year, Sarah Kueng and Lovis Caputo (winners in 2020) received a well-deserved Golden Hare award from *Hochparterre* magazine. We are also delighted to see a brand-new work by Rosmarie Tissi (winner in 2018), comprising 12 new alphabets, published by About Books.

This year's winners – Paola De Martin, Lucie Meier and Luciano Rigolini – are all trailblazers who have succeeded in questioning traditions. Read on to find out how their groundbreaking work has promoted diversity, inclusion, ethics, cooperation and technology in cultural circles. I hope you find their stories fascinating and, like every year, take inspiration from them for your own projects.

Anna Niederhäuser
Head of Design
Federal Office of Culture

[DE → p. 3, FR → p. 5]

Swiss Grand Award for Design Winners 2007–24

2024
Paola De Martin
  Designer and design researcher
Lucie Meier
  Fashion designer and creative director
Luciano Rigolini
  Photographer and producer for auteur documentary films

2023
Etienne Delessert
  Illustrator and graphic designer
Eleonore Peduzzi Riva
  Interior architect and consultant
Chantal Prod'Hom
  Museum director and curator

2022
Susanne Bartsch
  Talent curator and event producer
Verena Huber
  Interior architect
Beat Streuli
  Artist

2021
Julia Born
  Graphic designer
Peter Knapp
  Photographer and art director
Sarah Owens
  Design educator and researcher

2020
Ida Gut
  Fashion designer
Monique Jacot
  Photographer
Kueng Caputo
  Product designers

2019
Rosmarie Baltensweiler
  Product designer
Connie Hüsser
  Interior stylist
Thomi Wolfensberger
  Lithographer and publisher

2018
Cécile Feilchenfeldt
  Textile designer
Felco
  Product design
Rosmarie Tissi
  Graphic designer

2017
David Bielander
  Jewellery designer
Thomas Ott
  Illustrator
Jean Widmer
  Graphic designer and art director

2016
Claudia Caviezel
  Textile designer
Hans Eichenberger
  Product and interior designer
Ralph Schraivogel
  Graphic designer

2015
Luc Chessex
  Photographer
Lora Lamm
  Graphic designer
Team '77
  Typographers and type designers

2014
Erich Biehle
  Textile designer
Alfredo Häberli
  Furniture and product designer
Wolfgang Weingart
  Typographer

2013
Trix & Robert Haussmann
  Interior and product designers
Armin Hofmann
  Graphic designer
Martin Leuthold
  Textile designer

2012
Franco Clivio
  Product designer
Gavillet & Rust
  Graphic designers
Karl Gerstner
  Graphic designer

2011
Jörg Boner
  Product designer
NORM
  Graphic designers
Ernst Scheidegger
  Photographer
Walter Steiger
  Footwear designer

2010
Susi & Ueli Berger
  Furniture designers
Jean-Luc Godard
  Filmmaker
Sonnhild Kestler
  Textile designer
Otto Künzli
  Jewellery designer

2009
Robert Frank
  Photographer
Christoph Hefti
  Textile designer
Ursula Rodel
  Fashion designer
Thut Möbel
  Furniture design

2008
Holzer Kobler Architekturen
  Exhibition designers and architects
Albert Kriemler (Akris)
  Fashion designer
Alain Kupper
  Graphic designer, musician and artist
Walter Pfeiffer
  Photographer

2007
Ruth Grüninger
  Fashion designer
NOSE
  Communication design, service design
Bernhard Schobinger
  Jewellery designer
Adrian Frutiger
  Type desinger
Cornel Windlin
  Graphic designer

Swiss Federal Design Commission 2024

Chair
Nathalie Herschdorfer
  Director, Photo Élysée

Members
Cécile Feilchenfeldt
  Textile designer, Paris
Davide Fornari
  Professor for Research and Development at ECAL, Renens
David Glättli
  Industrial designer and creative director, Zurich/ Tokyo
Andreas Gysin
  Programmer and graphic designer, Lugano
Vera Sacchetti
  Design critic and curator, Basel
Ivan Sterzinger
  Graphic designer and publisher, Zurich

Colophon

Published on the occasion of the Swiss Grand Award for Design 2024

Head of project
  Anna Niederhäuser
  Federal Office of Culture (FOC), Bern

Editing, project coordination
  Mirjam Fischer
  mille pages, Zurich

Art direction and design
  Guillaume Chuard
  (Studio Ardworks),
  Lausanne / London

Typeface
  LL Geigy,
  Robert Huber / Lineto, Zurich

Photography (p. 7)
  © FOC / Diana Pfammatter

Translations
  Aurélie Duthoo (DE → FR)
  Silvia Giacomotti (DE/FR → IT)
  Lucas Moreno (IT → FR)
  Philippe Moser (FR / IT → DE)
  Mark O'Neil (FR → EN)
  Alain Perrinjaquet (DE → FR)
  Sarah Ponting (IT → EN)
  Annie Urselli (DE → IT)

Proofreading
  FOC Translation Services (DE / FR / IT)
  Mark O'Neil (EN)

Printing
  Gremper AG, Basel

Weitere Übersetzungen der Gespräche finden Sie auf:
Veuillez trouver les traductions françaises sur :
La traduzione italiana delle interviste è disponibile su:
www.schweizerkulturpreise.ch/design

© 2024 Federal Office of Culture, Bern and Verlag Scheidegger & Spiess AG, Zurich

Texts © the authors
Images © the artists

Verlag Scheidegger & Spiess
Niederdorfstrasse 54
8001 Zurich, Switzerland
www.scheidegger-spiess.ch

Scheidegger & Spiess is being supported by the Federal Office of Culture with a general subsidy for the years 2021–24.

All rights reserved; no part of this publication may be reproduced, stored in a retrieval system or transmitted in any form or by any means, electronic, mechanical, photocopying, recording, or otherwise, without the prior written consent of the publisher.

The three winners of the Swiss Grand Award for Design 2024 are: Paola De Martin, designer and design researcher, Lucie Meier, fashion designer and creative director, Luciano Rigolini, photographer and producer for auteur documentary film. The publication is distributed in a box containing three individual booklets – one for each winner – that are not available separately.

ISBN: 978-3-03942-207-4

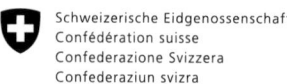

Schweizerische Eidgenossenschaft
Confédération suisse
Confederazione Svizzera
Confederaziun svizra

Eidgenössisches Departement des Innern EDI
Département fédéral de l'intérieur DFI
Dipartimento federale dell'interno DFI
Departament federal da l'intern DFI
Bundesamt für Kultur BAK
Office fédéral de la culture OFC
Ufficio federale della cultura UFC
Uffizi federal da cultura UFC

Schweizer Grand Prix Design

Grand Prix suisse de design   Gran Premio svizzero di design

Swiss Grand Award for Design

2024

Schweizer Grand Prix Design 2024

Der Schweizer Grand Prix Design zeichnet exemplarische Karrieren aus und bietet Sichtbarkeit für die Designschaffenden, deren Arbeit in der Sparte besonders interessante Wege und Gedankengänge eröffnet.

Welchen Stimmen wollen wir in einer Welt voller Lärm Gehör verschaffen? Sollen wir diejenigen würdigen, deren Arbeit dazu dient, unsere Objekte, Plakate, Webseiten oder Kleider schöner zu gestalten? Diejenigen, die sie nachhaltiger machen? Diejenigen, die Design als sozialen Akt verstehen? Kann Design überhaupt neue Botschaften vermitteln? Was bedeuten Denken und Kreieren im Jahr 2024, wenn die Welt in ihrer ganzen Vielfalt und Komplexität berücksichtigt wird?

Die Jury pflegt einen lebendigen Austausch zu diesen Fragen und misst der Botschaft, die sie mit der Wahl der Preisträgerinnen und Preisträger sendet, grösste Bedeutung bei. Es geht darum, die Arbeit von Einzelpersonen auszuzeichnen, die einen neuartigen, kreativen, engagierten Ansatz zur Anwendung bringen oder die Disziplin bedeutend geprägt haben und weiterhin prägen – selbstverständlich ohne dabei die Frauen zu vergessen, die besonders in der Vergangenheit weniger sichtbar waren. Ein Preis des Bundes, der von Kolleginnen und Kollegen aus der Sparte vergeben wird, würdigt auch Designschaffende, die die Grenzen ihrer Praxis ausloten.

2024 fiel die Wahl auf Persönlichkeiten, die in ihren Bereichen neue Wege beschreiten. Der Beitrag von Paola De Martin geht weit über die traditionelle Forschung hinaus. Mit ihren kritischen Betrachtungen bietet sie eine transdisziplinäre Herangehensweise an das Design, das sie in den gesellschaftlichen und politischen Kontext setzt. Bei ihr werden die Themen von Migration, Rassismus und gesellschaftlichem Ausschluss innerhalb der Disziplin betrachtet. Die Modedesignerin Lucie Meier hat in beeindruckender Geschwindigkeit international Karriere gemacht. Mit 40 Jahren arbeitet sie für grosse Häuser wie Louis Vuitton, Balenciaga, Dior oder Jil Sander. Wer seine Karriere im Ausland macht, erhält in der Schweiz oft spät Anerkennung. Mit Lucie Meier wollen wir eine Designerin würdigen, die über sichere und feine Kenntnisse ihres Handwerks verfügt. Luciano Rigolini hat mit seinen 74 Jahren nie damit aufgehört, die Bilder zu hinterfragen. Durch den Akt der Aneignung erforscht er sein Material und interessiert sich dabei besonders für triviale Fotografien, die unter seinem Blick neues plastisches Potenzial entfalten. Gleichzeitig verfolgte er eine internationale Karriere als Produzent von dokumentarischen Autorenfilmen.

Indem sie mit dem Schweizer Grand Prix Design 2024 Persönlichkeiten würdigt, die sich an unterschiedlichen Momenten ihres Berufslebens befinden und die alle ihren ganz eigenen Ansatz verfolgen, zeigt die Jury die vielen Perspektiven, die das Design eröffnet. Die Anerkennung für so verschiedene

Arbeitsweisen wie die von Paola De Martin, Lucie Meier und Luciano Rigolini unterstreicht die Vielfalt der möglichen Karrieren. Mit ihrer persönlichen Geschichte beweisen sie, dass es nicht nötig ist, einer Elite anzugehören, um Anerkennung zu erlangen. Denn die Grundsteine ihrer Kreativität sind Reflexion und Engagement.

Nathalie Herschdorfer, Präsidentin der Eidgenössischen Designkommission

Einleitung

Auch 18 Jahre nach der Lancierung der «höchsten Auszeichnung des Schweizer Designs» ist der Schweizer Grand Prix Design für das Bundesamt für Kultur (BAK) ein hervorragendes Instrument, um die Breite beruflicher Entwicklungswege und die Vielfalt im Design aufzuzeigen. Durch die Anerkennung unterschiedlicher Perspektiven und Herangehensweisen wird unser Blick auf die Bedeutung von Design in unserer Gesellschaft jedes Jahr reicher und dynamischer.

Der Preis wurde 2007 erstmals vergeben. Kurz davor wurden im BAK die «Projektbeiträge Design» eingestellt und die Eidgenössische Designkommission (EDnK) suchte nach neuen Wegen, die Designerinnen und Designer gezielter und proaktiver mit Fördergeldern zu unterstützen.

Im ersten Jahr wurden auf Vorschlag der EDnK fünf Preise vergeben, die von Beginn an mit je 40 000 Franken dotiert waren. Mit dem bedeutenden Schriftgestalter Adrian Frutiger und mit Bernhard Schobinger, einem der einflussreichsten Schmuckkünstler Europas, wurden international renommierte Persönlichkeiten ausgezeichnet. Mit der 1991 gegründeten Designagentur Nose, der Modedesignerin Ruth Grüninger und dem Grafiker Cornel Windlin, damals knapp 40-jährig, kam zudem eine jüngere Generation zum Zug. Ziel des BAK war es, Designschaffenden zu ermöglichen, an innovativen Projekten zu arbeiten und ihr kreatives Potenzial weiterzuentwickeln, ohne sich ausschliesslich auf den kommerziellen Erfolg konzentrieren zu müssen.

Die Auszeichnungen prägen ein Stück Schweizer Designgeschichte. Die dazu erscheinende Publikation beinhaltet oftmals erste Sichtungen von Archiven und dient als Basis für künftige Werkpräsentationen und Forschungsarbeiten. Gerade im vergangenen Jahr bekamen zahlreiche ehemalige Preisträgerinnen des Schweizer Grand Prix Design (SGPD) eine eigene Plattform: Im Landesmuseum war eine monografische Ausstellung über das Ausnahmetalent im Schweizer Modedesign Ursula Rodel (SGPD 2009) zu entdecken. Über die Leuchtendesign-Pionierin Rosmarie Baltensweiler (2019) erschien im letzten September ein umfangreicher Werkkatalog, Eleonore Peduzzi Riva (2023), die weit mehr als das weltberühmte DS-600-Sofa mitentwickelt hat, wurde an Panels eingeladen und mehrfach interviewt, im Museum für Gestaltung Zürich konnte man jüngst die textilen Wunderwerke von Claudia Caviezel (2016) geniessen und Sarah Kueng und Lovis Caputo (2020) erhielten Ende 2023 den wohlverdienten Goldenen Hasen von Hochparterre. Und aktuell freuen wir uns über eine Publikation mit zwölf neuen Alphabeten von Rosmarie Tissi (2018), die im Verlag About Books erscheint.

Die diesjährigen Preisträgerinnen Paola De Martin und Lucie Meier sowie den Preisträger Luciano Rigolini verbindet die Fähigkeit, Traditionen zu hinterfragen und neue Wege zu beschreiten. Wie die drei mit ihrem innovativen Schaffen dazu beitragen, Vielfalt, Inklusion, Ethik, Zusammenarbeit und Technologie in der Kultur zu fördern, können Sie, liebe Leserin, lieber Leser, nun bei der Lektüre erfahren. Ich wünsche Ihnen viele spannende Entdeckungen und wie jedes Jahr auch viel Inspiration für Ihre eigenen Projekte.

Anna Niederhäuser
Leitung Design
Bundesamt für Kultur

Grand Prix suisse de design 2024

Le Grand Prix suisse de design distingue des carrières exemplaires et offre une visibilité à des créatrices et des créateurs dont le travail ouvre une voie ou des réflexions particulièrement intéressantes dans ce domaine.

Quelles voix faire entendre dans un monde aussi bruyant que le nôtre ? Faut-il valoriser celles et ceux qui conçoivent des créations destinées à rendre nos objets, nos affiches, nos sites Internet, nos vêtements plus beaux ? Celles et ceux qui les rendent plus durables ? Celles et ceux qui voient dans le design un acte social ? Le design peut-il être porteur de nouveaux messages ? Que signifie, en 2024, penser et créer tout en tenant compte de la diversité et de la complexité de notre monde ?

Le jury échange activement autour de ces questions et considère avec la plus grande attention le message qu'il souhaite transmettre en distinguant trois lauréat-e-s. Il s'agit de valoriser le travail d'individus à l'approche novatrice, créatrice ou engagée, ou encore qui exercent ou qui ont exercé une influence marquante dans leur discipline. Ceci, bien sûr, sans oublier les femmes, qui dans le passé ont souvent été reléguées à l'arrière plan. L'annonce des Grands Prix attire l'attention des médias et permet de parler des différents domaines du design à un public varié. Un prix fédéral, décerné par des pairs, rend aussi hommage à des professionnels qui explorent les contours de leur pratique.

En 2024, le choix s'est porté sur des personnes qui ont choisi un chemin novateur dans leur domaine. La contribution de Paola De Martin dépasse largement la recherche traditionnelle. Par ses réflexions critiques, elle offre une approche transdisciplinaire au design qu'elle intègre dans un contexte social et politique. Chez elle, les questions de migration, de racisme et d'exclusion sociale s'invitent dans la discipline. La créatrice de mode Lucie Meier mène une carrière internationale fulgurante. À 40 ans, elle a travaillé pour de grandes maisons, parmi lesquelles Louis Vuitton, Balenciaga, Dior et Jil Sander. Pour celles et ceux qui développent une carrière à l'étranger, la reconnaissance arrive souvent de façon tardive. Avec Lucie Meier, il s'agit de valoriser une créatrice qui a de solides et sensibles connaissances dans son métier. Enfin, Luciano Rigolini est à 74 ans un créateur qui n'a jamais cessé d'interroger les images. C'est par l'acte d'appropriation qu'il explore sa matière, s'intéressant particulièrement aux photographies vernaculaires. Sous son regard, les photographies dévoilent de nouvelles potentialités plastiques. En parallèle il a mené une carrière internationale comme producteur dans le domaine du film documentaire d'auteur.

En réunissant autour du Grand Prix suisse de design 2024, des individus se trouvant à différents moments de leur vie professionnelle et qui témoignent chacun-e d'une approche singulière, le jury signifie que le design ouvre de nombreuses perspectives. Reconnaître le travail de Paola De Martin, de Lucie

Meier et de Luciano Rigolini dont les pratiques sont relativement éloignées l'une de l'autre, permet de montrer des voies multiples. À travers leur histoire personnelle, on voit qu'il n'est pas nécessaire d'appartenir à une élite pour aspirer à la reconnaissance, car le ciment de leur créativité réside dans la réflexion et l'engagement.

Nathalie Herschdorfer, Présidente de la Commission fédérale de design

Introduction

Dix-huit ans après la création de la « plus prestigieuse distinction du design suisse », le Grand Prix suisse de design de l'Office fédéral de la culture (OFC) demeure un remarquable instrument qui permet de mettre en évidence la diversité du design et celle des parcours professionnels dans le domaine. En reconnaissant des perspectives et des approches différentes, nous pouvons d'année en année porter un regard de plus en plus riche et dynamique sur l'importance du design dans notre société.

C'est en 2007 que le prix a été décerné pour la première fois. Peu de temps auparavant, l'OFC avait cessé d'octroyer ses « contributions à des projets de design » et la Commission fédérale de design était à la recherche de nouvelles manières de soutenir les designers par des aides ciblées et proactives.

La première année, cinq prix ont été décernés sur proposition de la CFD ; comme aujourd'hui, chacun d'eux était doté d'une somme de 40 000 francs. Ils couronnaient, d'une part, des personnalités de renommée internationale, comme Adrian Frutiger, important créateur de caractères d'imprimerie, et Bernhard Schobinger, un des plus influents bijoutiers d'art d'Europe. Mais ils faisaient aussi une place à la nouvelle génération, avec l'agence de design Nose, fondée en 1991, la créatrice de mode Ruth Grüninger et le graphiste Cornel Windlin, alors tout juste quarantenaire. Le but de l'OFC était de permettre à des designers de travailler à des projets novateurs et de développer leurs potentialités créatives sans qu'ils soient contraints de se concentrer sur le succès commercial.

Les prix décernés sont le reflet de tout un pan de l'histoire du design suisse. Souvent, la publication qui les accompagne donne un aperçu des archives des lauréats qui sera un point de départ pour des rétrospectives et des travaux de recherche ultérieurs. L'année dernière, nombre d'anciens lauréats du Grand Prix suisse de design ont été mis sur le devant de la scène. Le Musée national suisse a ainsi consacré une exposition monographique à Ursula Rodel (Grand Prix 2009), créatrice de mode d'un exceptionnel talent, tandis qu'un riche catalogue de l'œuvre de Rosmarie Baltensweiler (2019), pionnière du design de luminaires, paraissait en septembre dernier. Dans le même temps, Eleonore Peduzzi Riva (2023), dont le canapé DS-600, mondialement connu, n'est de loin pas la seule création, courait les tables rondes et les entretiens, et le Musée du design de Zurich accueillait les merveilleuses œuvres textiles de Claudia Caviezel (2016), alors que la revue Hochparterre attribuait à Sarah Kueng et Lovis Caputo (2020) une distinction amplement méritée, le Goldener Hase, et que, tout récemment, nous pouvions nous réjouir de la parution aux éditions About Books de douze nouveaux alphabets de Rosmarie Tissi (2018).

Les deux lauréates et le lauréat de cette année, Paola De Martin, Lucie Meier et Luciano Rigolini, s'apparentent par leur capacité de remettre en question les traditions et de s'engager dans de nouvelles voies. Dans les pages qui suivent, vous apprendrez comment ces trois créateurs innovants promeuvent une culture basée sur la diversité, l'inclusion, l'éthique, la coopération et la technologie. Je vous souhaite de faire des découvertes captivantes et d'y puiser, comme chaque année, une riche inspiration pour vos propres projets.

Anna Niederhäuser
Responsable design
Office fédéral de la culture

[IT → p. 43, EN → p. 45]

Paola De Martin

Paola De Martin
Avanti guanti – Die neue Avantgarde ist bereit!

von Francesca Petrarca

Paola ist mir auf einem Foto begegnet, bevor ich wusste, wo sie steht. Ihre Blogs habe ich gelesen, bevor ich wusste, wie sie spricht. Als ich ihre Stimme dann im Radio gehört habe, war ich ergriffen von dem, was sie sagt. Paola De Martin bewegt: sich, mich und andere. Sie ist eine «scholar activist», ihr Werdegang ein Muster für sich. Ihre Praxis ist verknüpfende aktivistische Designforschung, welche die verschwiegenen Zusammenhänge von Ästhetik, Gesellschaft und Klasse untersucht. Vom Schweigen hat sie sich in zahlreichen Publikationen verabschiedet. In friedlichen Aktionen findet sie passende Formen für ihren Protest. Den aufgeladenen sozialen Kontexten der Gegenwart begegnet sie mit symbolischer Abrüstung. Immer neugierig, niemals allein.

Da ist stets diese Masche, die alles verbindet. Paolas Arbeitsweise ist von Literatur, Kunst und Design geprägt, sie verbindet Geschichte und Soziologie mit Gestaltung, ist anderen Menschen zugewandt: eine ineinanderfliessende Metamorphose, die in Gegenständen, Performances, Lectures, Briefen, Fotos, Musik, Hörspielen, Essays, Artikeln mündet. In ihrer Lehre an Hochschulen für Gestaltung und als Postdoc an der ETH erfährt Paola grossen Zulauf von Studierenden. Sie lehrt, über Ausgrenzungen zu reflektieren und ermutigt, sich intersektional mit der sozialen Herkunft und mit Privilegien zu beschäftigen. Als Dozentin mit «impact» ist ihre Reflexion über Normen, Regeln, Strukturen eine wegweisende Auseinandersetzung für andere. Sie setzt kritische Akzente und gibt Impulse an die junge Designgeneration weiter. Der mündliche Ausdruck befruchtet das verschriftlichte Nachdenken und umgekehrt. Aus der «Einsamkeit der Langstreckenläuferin» wuchs, dank der Zusammenarbeit mit dem Kollektiv vom Schwarzenbach-Komplex, ein freundschaftliches Gewebe. Das öffentliche Interesse an der Aufarbeitung der Schweizer Familienpolitik im Namen des von ihr initiierten Vereins TESORO ist gross. Paola schlägt die gesellschaftlichen Fäden auf ihren Zaubernadeln an, in ihren Händen werden die Maschen neu verknüpft.

Wenn das Private politisch ist, wie die frühen Feministinnen sagten, dann stellt Paola die Frage ins Zentrum: Wie politisch ist *Ästhetik*? Paola hat mir selbstgestrickte Handschuhe geschenkt, mit einem aufwändigen Muster, in grün und rosa. Durch das Stricken kann sie ihre Gedanken ordnen, kann innere Kraft schöpfen, wenn es draussen kalt und zynisch ist. Der konstruktive Widerstand ist tief in ihr verwurzelt. Eine Erinnerung aus Paolas Primarschulzeit in Zürich-Affoltern: die Handarbeitslehrerin verbietet der jungen Paola das Stricken auf «italienische» Art, denn die sei nicht so, wie diejenige, welche die Lehrerin ausführe und überhaupt, wenn Paola einen «italienischen» Fehler mache, so könne sie ihr nicht helfen. Doch zum Glück hat Paola, zuerst heimlich, beide Techniken miteinander verknüpft und das Verknüpfen später zu ihrem Leitmotiv gemacht.

Durch die Doktorarbeit «Give us a break! Arbeitermilieu und Designszene im Aufbruch» (Diaphanes, 2020) hat sich Paolas Zunge langsam wie ein Teppich ausgerollt: Die gefundene Sprache hat Platz geschaffen, die bislang ungehörten Geschichten zu artikulieren. Paola beschäftigt sich mit dem Gefühl von Zugehörigkeit und Nicht-Zugehörigkeit zum Zürcher Designfeld, wo sie in den 1990er-Jahren als Textilstudentin und später als Mitbegründerin des Modelabels Beige tätig war. Ausgangspunkt sind Erfahrungen, die sie aufgrund ihrer sozialen Herkunft aus einer bildungssystemfernen, migrantischen Arbeiterfamilie machte. Am Ende hat sie die historischen Verzerrungen im Design, die sie einst orientierungslos machten, aufgespürt. Das Nicht-Gesagte, das wie ein «Elefant» im Raum steht und von den «Erben des kulturellen Kapitals» ignoriert wird, hat Paola präzise angeschaut. Sie selbst exponiert sich als Forscherin, geht selbstreflektiert mit ihren eigenen Verstrickungen, ihren Diskriminierungen *und* Privilegien um. Paola greift sowohl auf Theorie als auch auf autobiografische Literatur zurück und fügt alles zu einem dichten Beziehungsgewebe zusammen. Die Arbeit beleuchtet das System, in dem wir als Designschaffende drin sind. Sie ist eine manifeste Kritik an den bestehenden Strukturen, die Menschen mit unterprivilegierter Klassenherkunft reflexartig aus dem Feld ausschliessen, sie schubladisieren und andere bevorzugen und weitertragen.

Die Strophen dieses Manifests sind wie die farbigen Fäden meiner Handschuhe. Der Protest im Weiterstricken, trotz Mahnung der Lehrerin, es

1. Belege: Mali Lazell, Julia Haenni: ICH WILL ALLES! Streikporträts, edition clandestin 2021, o. S.; «Brennende Unschärfe – Offener Brief an Bundesrätin Simonetta Sommaruga», Institut Neue Schweiz INES, Blog, 21.9.2018; «Per arrivare bisogna partire», Institut Neue Schweiz INES, Blog, 4.11.2019; «Saisonnierstatut: Das war ein Attentat auf die Familien» (SRF 2 Kultur, «Kontext», 7.12.2021).

doch gefälligst «richtig» zu machen. Der Protest der Eltern, das Kleinkind Paola, trotz Landesverweis der Fremdenpolizei, zurück in die Schweiz zu holen. Der Protest des Nicht-mehr-Schweigens. Die Faust, die sich im Kampf um Gerechtigkeit langsam öffnet: Es fängt mit einer «falschen» Masche an und formiert sich zu einem widerständigen Handschuh, der seinesgleichen sucht. Vorwärts gehen sie, unsere Erinnerungen, Hand in Hand: Meine *nonna* zeigte mir einst ihre aufwändigen, selbstgehäkelten Handschuhe, elegante *guanti*, die sie zum Spazieren in Italien und später in der Schweiz trug. Leider sind sie verloren gegangen. Der Verlust wiegt schwerer als man denken könnte. Er hallt im weitervererbten Gefühl des Verlusts meiner *nonna* wider, die in der Schweiz nicht mit ihrem Kind, meiner Mutter, zusammenleben durfte. Paolas Handschuhe beginnen, diese Wunde zu heilen. Aus meinen «bestrickten» Händen wird ein Zauberlied, aus den Maschenreihen ein in den Bann ziehender Refrain. Dieser magische Rhythmus setzt Energie frei, wird ein Fluss, der vorwärts strömt.

Es ist kein Zufall, dass eine Designerin mit «Migrationsvorsprung» die Frage stellt: *Wie* politisch ist Ästhetik? Paola öffnet einen Reflexionsraum, wo vorher keiner war, lädt uns ein, über Klassismus und andere Diskriminierungs*formen* in unserer Kultur nachzudenken. Sie wagt einen mutigen Schritt vom «Ich» zum «Wir», wenn sie betont: «Wir können nichts dafür, in welche Klasse wir hineingeboren werden, aber wir können die ästhetischen Urteile und Reflexe, die aus diesem Zufall heraus entstehen, verstehen, vermitteln – und, wenn wir wollen, sogar verändern.» *Avanti guanti* – Die neue Avantgarde ist bereit!

Francesca Petrarca studierte Kunstgeschichte, Medienwissenschaften, Visuelle Kommunikation sowie Bildforschung in Basel und arbeitet als selbstständige Buchgestalterin. Ihr Buch No grazie, non fumo ist ein literarisches und gestalterisches Porträt der Migrationsgeschichte ihrer Grossmutter und erscheint 2024 in der 2. Auflage im Verlag edition clandestin.

Paola De Martin

Avanti guanti – la nouvelle avant-garde est prête !

par Francesca Petrarca

J'ai vu Paola sur une photo avant de savoir qui elle était. J'ai lu ses blogs avant de savoir comment elle parlait. Plus tard, quand j'ai entendu sa voix à la radio, j'ai été touchée par ce qu'elle disait [1]. Paola De Martin bouge, se déplace, évolue, entraîne les autres – et moi. C'est une « activiste universitaire », son parcours lui-même semble taillé selon un patron. Sa pratique est une recherche activiste et intégrative sur le design qui étudie les liens non-dits entre esthétique, société et classes sociales. Se taire : une attitude à laquelle elle a tourné le dos par de nombreuses publications. À travers des actions pacifiques, elle trouve des formes adaptées à sa contestation. Au contexte social explosif de notre époque, elle répond par un désarmement symbolique. Toujours curieuse, jamais seule.

Il y a toujours cette maille qui relie tout. La méthode de travail de Paola est marquée par la littérature, l'art et le design, elle combine histoire, sociologie et création, et elle est tournée vers les autres : c'est une métamorphose toute en fluidité, qui débouche sur des objets, des performances, des lectures, des lettres, des photos, de la musique, des pièces radiophoniques, des essais et des articles. Les cours que donne Paola dans les hautes écoles de design et en postdoc à l'ETH attirent beaucoup d'étudiants. Elle leur apprend à réfléchir aux processus d'exclusion et les encourage à se préoccuper de l'origine sociale et des privilèges dans une optique intersectionnelle. Chargée de cours « à fort impact », elle mène une réflexion sur les normes, les règles, les structures qui montre la voie à suivre. Avec un regard souvent critique, elle transmet des impulsions nouvelles à la jeune génération du design. L'expression orale féconde la réflexion poursuivie à l'écrit, et inversement. Grâce à la collaboration avec le collectif du Schwarzenbach-Komplex, la « solitude de la coureuse de fond » s'est muée en tissu d'amitiés. Le public manifeste beaucoup d'intérêt pour la relec-

---

1. Preuves : Mali Lazell, Julia Haenni: ICH WILL ALLES! Streikporträts, edition clandestin 2021, s. p.; « Brennende Unschärfe – Offener Brief an Bundesrätin Simonetta Sommaruga », Institut Neue Schweiz INES, blog, 21.9.2018 ; « Per arrivare bisogna partire », Institut Neue Schweiz INES, blog, 4.11.2019; « Saisonnierstatut: Das war ein Attentat auf die Familien » (SRF 2 Kultur, « Kontext », 7.12.2021)

ture critique de la politique familiale suisse exigée par l'association Tesoro, qu'elle a fondée. Paola s'empare des fils de la société pour monter des mailles sur ses aiguilles magiques : sous ses doigts, un nouveau tricot prend forme.

Si le privé est politique, comme l'affirmaient les premières féministes, alors Paola met cette question sur la table : à quel point l'*esthétique* est-elle politique ? Paola m'a offert des gants tricotés main dans un subtil jacquard vert et rose. Tricoter lui permet de mettre ses idées en ordre, de reprendre des forces quand le monde extérieur est froid et cynique. En elle, la résistance constructive est profondément enracinée. Souvenir de l'époque où Paola allait à l'école primaire à Zurich-Affoltern : la professeure de travaux manuels interdisait à Paola de tricoter « à l'italienne », car ce n'était pas la façon de faire de l'enseignante, et si Paola faisait une erreur « italienne », elle disait qu'elle ne pourrait pas l'aider. Heureusement, Paola a combiné les deux techniques (d'abord en secret), et par la suite, ce principe de combinaison est devenu son leitmotiv.

Avec sa thèse « Give us a break ! Arbeitermilieu und Designszene im Aufbruch » (Diaphanes, 2020), la langue de Paola s'est peu à peu déroulée comme un tapis : le langage qu'elle a trouvé a créé la place nécessaire pour exprimer les histoires que jusqu'ici nul n'entendait. Paola s'intéresse au sentiment d'appartenance et de non-appartenance au milieu du design zurichois, qu'elle a fréquenté dans les années 1990 lorsqu'elle était étudiante en textile, puis en tant que cofondatrice de la marque de mode Beige. Son point de départ, ce sont ses propres expériences dues à ses origines sociales : Paola vient d'une famille ouvrière immigrée éloignée du système éducatif. À l'arrivée, elle a mis le doigt sur les biais historiques dans le design qui auparavant la désorientaient. Le non-dit, cet « éléphant » dans la pièce, ignoré par les « héritiers du capital culturel », Paola l'a regardé de près. Elle-même s'expose en tant que chercheuse, réfléchit à ses propres intrications, aux discriminations qu'elle subit *et* aux privilèges dont elle jouit. Paola recourt tout autant à la théorie qu'à la littérature autobiographique et assemble tous ces éléments en un tissu relationnel serré. De fil en aiguille, son travail met en lumière le système dont nous, designers, faisons partie. C'est une critique manifeste des structures en place, qui tendent à exclure automatiquement du champ les personnes issues de classes défavorisées, à les mettre à l'écart, à en préférer et à en favoriser d'autres.

Les strophes de ce manifeste sont comme les fils colorés de mes gants. La protestation de la petite fille qui continue à tricoter malgré les remontrances de la maîtresse qui lui demande de bien vouloir le faire « correctement ». La protestation des parents qui ramènent en Suisse Paola encore bébé malgré l'expulsion ordonnée par la police des étrangers. La protestation de celles et ceux qui ne veulent plus se taire. Le poing qui s'ouvre lentement à force de lutter pour la justice : ça commence par une maille « mal montée », et ça devient un gant rebelle, qui cherche son pareil. Ils avancent, nos souvenirs, main dans la main : un jour, ma *nonna* m'avait montré ses gants, très travaillés, crochetés par ses soins, d'élégants *guanti* qu'elle portait en Italie pour la promenade, et plus tard en Suisse. Malheureusement, ils se sont perdus. Une perte plus lourde qu'on pourrait le penser. Elle fait écho à ce sentiment dont j'ai hérité, le sentiment de perte de ma *nonna*, à qui on a interdit de vivre en Suisse avec son enfant – ma mère. Les gants de Paola commencent à guérir cette blessure. De mes mains « entricotées » s'élève un chant merveilleux, et des rangs de mailles, un refrain enchanteur. Ce rythme magique libère des énergies, tout un fleuve, dont le cours s'impose.

Ce n'est pas un hasard si c'est une designer riche de son passé migratoire qui pose cette question : à quel point l'esthétique est-elle politique ? Paola ouvre un espace de réflexion entièrement vierge, nous invite à réfléchir au classisme et à d'autres formes de discrimination dans notre culture. Elle ose faire un pas courageux du « je » au « nous » quand elle insiste : « Nous ne pouvons rien au hasard qui nous a fait naître dans telle ou telle classe sociale, mais nous pouvons comprendre les jugements et les réflexes esthétiques qui en résultent, les transmettre, et même, si nous le voulons, les changer. » *Avanti guanti* – la nouvelle avant-garde est prête !

Francesca Petrarca a étudié l'histoire de l'art, les sciences des médias, la communication visuelle et la science des images à Bâle. Elle est graphiste-conceptrice de livres indépendante. No grazie, non fumo, ouvrage littéraire et graphique dans lequel elle raconte la trajectoire migratoire de sa grand-mère, est réédité en 2024 par edition clandestin.

[IT → p. 37, EN → p. 38]

Working class appropriation
Classplaining
Othering
Silencing
Classfluidity
Legitimate
Illegal
High-trash

Klasse
Klassenfrage
Klassengrenze
Klassenflucht
Klassensolidarität
Klassenkonversion
Klassenherkunft
Klassendünkel
Klassenblindheit
Klassensäuberung
Klassensafari
Klassenzärtlichkeit

Class
Class question
Class boundary
Class flight
Class solidarity
Class conversion
Class heredity
Class conceit
Class blindness
Class cleansing
Class safari
Class tenderness

Translated from the German

Clivage de l'habitus
La distinction de la distinction
Snobisme
Implicite-explicite
Réfléchie-réflexive
Naturalisation
Post-post moderne

Cleavage of the habitus
The distinction of distinction
Snobbery
Implicit-explicit
Reflective-reflexive
Naturalisation
Post-post modern

Translated from the French

PP. 15 – 19, 30 – 38   These word lists are products of a joint terminology effort. Paola De Martin and Francesca Petrarca finalised them after their conversation, which can be found in the brochure on pages 22 – 31. They are living vessels that encapsulate the semantic force fields at the heart of Paola's craft, thought, research and activism.

PP. 20, 33   Encompassing literature, art and design, her way of working creates links to history and sociology and is always turned towards others. It is an intertwining metamorphosis that produces objects, performances, lectures, letters, photos, music, radio plays, essays and articles.

[DE] FRANCESCA PETRARCA IM GESPRÄCH MIT PAOLA DE MARTIN, DEZEMBER 2023

Francesca Petrarca: Liebe Paola, mir fällt auf, dass Du so treffende Bilder verwendest. Du sprichst zum Beispiel von einer «Schere im Kopf, die ständig gewisse Gedanken und Geschichten abschneidet.»

Paola De Martin: Das sagen mir viele, dass ich mit passenden Metaphern argumentieren kann. Das ist mir nicht bewusst. Mein Habitus vielleicht? Meine spontane Art, Menschen zu erreichen, die weniger formelle Bildung haben als ich? Viele, die *Give us a break!* gelesen haben, sagen mir, dass es ein schwieriges und schweres Buch sei, aber auch, dass sie sich immer angesprochen und mitgenommen gefühlt haben.

FP: Deine als Buch veröffentlichte Dissertation ist sehr zugänglich. Die Lesenden können immer wieder an ihrem eigenen Leben anknüpfen. Das Buch beinhaltet sowohl Anekdoten – Du nennst sie soziale Muster – als auch selbstreflexive Analysen, Gespräche mit anderen Designschaffenden, und immer wieder machst Du Bezüge zu Literatur, Kunst, Kultur und Forschung. Du hast eine Sprache gefunden, um Deine Forschung möglichst nahbar wiederzugeben. Was sind weitere Reaktionen, wenn Du über Klasse und soziale Herkunft sprichst?

PDM: In meinen Seminaren sind vor allem, aber nicht nur, die Studierenden aus wenig privilegierten Milieus oft sehr bewegt. Sie sagen mir manchmal unter Tränen, dass sie gar nicht wussten, dass das, was sie fühlten, eine Sprache hat und dass so darüber nachgedacht werden kann.

FP: Womit hängt das zusammen?

PDM: In der Schweiz hat es vermutlich damit zu tun, dass Klasse und Diskriminierung keine Themen sind, über die man einen öffentlichkeitswirksamen Diskurs pflegt. Sehr oft heisst es: «Rassismus gibt es in der Schweiz gar nicht». Oder auch: «Wir sind keine Klassengesellschaft.» Erst langsam fängt eine Aufarbeitung der tiefen Strukturen von Rassismus an. Klassendünkel und mehr oder weniger subtiler Hass als Ausgrenzung gegen Menschen in prekären Situationen ist hingegen noch unsichtbarer und unbenannter.

FP: Hängt das mangelnde Bewusstsein für die Klassenunterschiede und deren Auswirkungen auf die Gesellschaft vielleicht auch damit zusammen, dass es in der Schweiz keine so grosse Tradition von autobiografischer Literatur gibt wie zum Beispiel in Frankreich mit Annie Ernaux und Édouard Louis?

PDM: Die Tradition, die Pierre Bourdieu mit seiner «auto-socio-biographie» begründet hat, auf die sich diese Autor:innen explizit beziehen, ist ein ganz spezieller Zugang, der sehr reflektiert ist, und immer auch zurückgeht in die eigene Erfahrung. Er verknüpft Theorie mit Empirie. Autor:innen, die mit autobiografischen Bezügen operieren, gibt es hierzulande schon, aber die gesellschaftliche Kritik wird weniger explizit artikuliert und theoretisch auch weniger soziologisch verankert. Ich wollte die Designszene an diese Denktradition andocken – aus zwei Gründen: Weil die Kulturbranche im Spätkapitalismus so stark gewachsen ist. Und ich wollte das

«Klassendünkel und mehr oder weniger subtiler Hass als Ausgrenzung gegen Menschen in prekären Situationen ist hingegen noch unsichtbarer und unbenannter.»

kritisch reflektieren, weil ich den Reflexionsraum vermisst habe und weil ich diese Kultur der coolen, postmodernen, trashigen Distinktion – also Abgrenzung gegen unten mittels Geschmack – eine Zumutung finde.

FP: Wie steht es denn um die Forschung zum Thema Klasse und Herkunft in der Schweiz?

PDM: Ich finde es erstaunlich, dass viele Forschende zu Klasse und Kultur lieber über ein anderes Land forschen als über die Schweiz. Es gibt auch viele Leute aus dem internationalen, akademischen Kontext, die mir sagen: «Ich dachte, in der Schweiz gäbe es gar keine

[EN] FRANCESCA PETRARCA IN CONVERSATION WITH PAOLA DE MARTIN, DECEMBER 2023

Francesca Petrarca: My dear Paola, I'm struck by how you use such fitting imagery. For example, you talk about a "pair of scissors in the mind, constantly snipping off certain thoughts and stories".
Paola De Martin: A lot of people tell me that I'm good at finding the right metaphors to back up my arguments. I don't do it consciously. Perhaps it's just my habitus, my spontaneous way of getting through to people who haven't had as much formal education as me. Many who have read *Give us a break!* tell me that it's a difficult read, heavy going but also involving, and that it really spoke to them.
FP: Your dissertation, which was published as a book, is very accessible. Readers can relate a lot of it to their own lives, and it contains not only anecdotes – you call them social patterns – but

"[…] whereas the classism and hate – however subtle – that marginalise the underprivileged remain unseen and unspoken."

also self-analysis and discussions with other designers, not to mention plenty of references to literature, art, culture and research. You've found a voice that draws people into your research. What other reactions do you get when you talk about class and social background?
PDM: In my seminars, it's mainly (although not exclusively) the students from less privileged backgrounds who are moved a lot. They sometimes tell me through tears that they had no idea there was a language to express and think about what they felt.
FP: Where does that come from?
PDM: In Switzerland, it probably comes from the lack of public discourse on class and discrimination. You often hear "There's no racism in Switzerland," or even "We're a classless society." The country is only just starting to examine its deeply embedded structural racism, whereas the classism and hate – however subtle – that marginalise the underprivileged remain unseen and unspoken.
FP: Could the lack of awareness of class differences and their impact on society perhaps be explained by Switzerland not having such a great tradition of autobiographical literature as France, for example, does with Annie Ernaux and Édouard Louis?
PDM: The tradition Pierre Bourdieu started with his "auto-socio-biography", to which these two authors explicitly refer, is a very special, highly reflexive approach that always draws on personal experience. It links theory and empirical observation. We do have authors who use autobiographical elements in Switzerland, but social critiques are less explicitly articulated and less rooted in sociological theory. I wanted to connect the design scene to this thought tradition for two reasons. The sector of cultural production has grown so big in the era of late-stage capitalism, and I wanted to reflect on that critically because I didn't see any existing space for reflection. Also, I can't stand this culture of cool, postmodern, trashy distinction – marginalisation through taste, if you will.
FP: Has Switzerland made any progress in research on class and social background?
PDM: I'm astounded that so many people researching class and culture prefer to focus on other countries rather than Switzerland. There are also a lot of academics from other countries who say to me, "I didn't think there was a working class in Switzerland." I speak out in favour of studying Switzerland and its history: the social history of Swiss architecture, art, design, literature and

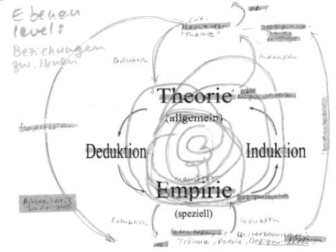

A. University of the Arts Bern, input on theory and empirical observation

FP: Arbeiter:innen.» Ich mache mich sehr stark dafür, dass wir die Schweiz und ihre Geschichte anschauen: die Sozialgeschichte der Schweizer Architektur-, Kunst-, Design-, Literatur- und Theaterszene. Da gibt es noch unendlich viel Material, mit dem man arbeiten könnte. Gerade jetzt entdeckt man die koloniale Vergangenheit der Schweiz. Und diese hat auch einen Genderaspekt, der wiederum eine Klassenvergangenheit und -gegenwart hat. Warum also die Schweiz immer aussen vor lassen?

FP: Kommt das vom Klischee, dass alle in der Schweiz «reich» seien?

PDM: Wahrscheinlich. Ich finde es mittlerweile auch ein Klischee zu sagen, die Schweiz habe im Zweiten Weltkrieg keinen Schaden davongetragen. Aber wer hat den Preis gezahlt für diese schadlose Schweiz? Da wird vieles verdrängt. Der brutale Umgang mit Verdingkindern und den Familien von Jenischen, Sinti und Rom bis weit in die 1970er-Jahre, die abgewiesenen jüdischen Flüchtlinge und der brutale Kunsthandel mit ihrem Besitz, bis hin zum ganzen Überfremdungsdiskurs. Irgendjemand musste für die Schadlosen bezahlen. Nicht zuletzt die Frauen, die so spät politisch integriert wurden.

FP: Die Wahrnehmung dieser Zusammenhänge und der Geschichte hat mit der Sprache zu tun, oder? Ivna Žic spricht davon in ihrem Buch *Wahrscheinliche Herkünfte*. Sie weist darauf hin, dass wir einander neue Fragen stellen sollten. Dass also nicht mehr gefragt wird: «Woher kommst Du?»

PDM: Ja, das finde ich grundsätzlich auch, wobei, wenn man an die *soziale* Herkunft denkt, dann hat die Frage ja einen anderen Subtext, oder? Und es ist äusserst produktiv zu fragen, aus welcher Klasse jemand kommt, das mache ich in meinen Seminaren regelmässig.

Ich weiss gar nicht, ob es um die Sprache an sich geht, oder vielmehr um ein Reflektieren mit sprachlichen Mitteln, also um eine Haltung. Wofür brauche ich die Sprache? Wieso ist das kollektive Verschweigen von Klassenfragen im Kopf dermassen stark in diesem Land, dass es mir nicht erlaubt ist, gewisse Dinge überhaupt zu benennen? Ich bin oft mit einer tief verankerten Intellektuellenfeindlichkeit konfrontiert, die zu Blockaden führt. Das scheint mir ein wichtiger blinder Punkt zu sein. Denn Sprache und Virtuosität gibt es ja schon. Wir haben Literaturschaffende. Aber gewisse Themen werden einfach nicht berührt. Und da habe ich eine Lust verspürt auf diese «low hanging fruits». So im Stil von: Was passiert, wenn ich mit meiner Zunge dort hingehe und beschreibe, wie sie schmecken? Das Schreiben darüber hat mir viel Befriedigung gegeben. Da fand ich es auch spannend, mit der Zeit und mit einer gewissen Routine zu merken: Bourdieu ist gut, aber irgendwann komme ich mit seinem Argumentarium auch an eine Grenze. Ich bekam Lust, weiterzugehen und die Analysebegriffe zu verfeinern – anhand der queerfeministischen und postkolonialen Theorie zum Beispiel.

FP: Welche Analysebegriffe meinst Du?

PDM: Ich habe gemerkt, dass die Kultursoziologie tendenziell bei der Erfahrung der Scham haftenbleibt. Im Lexikon der Soziologie ist der Begriff «Stolz» nicht drin, dafür gibt es für «Scham» und «Schuld» sehr lange Artikel. Mir war zwar schon sehr wichtig, was Annie Ernaux gesagt hat: In der Scham, in der Demütigung sind die sozialen Details sehr scharf erkennbar. Darum ist die Scham eine Art persönliches Medium für die Erforschung gesellschaftlicher Strukturen der Ungleichheit. Durch die Scham gehst du wieder ganz genau dorthin, wo Theorie und Praxis sich berühren. Für die kollektive Geschichte kann man viel Wertvolles aus diesen

«Ich bekam Lust, weiterzugehen und die Analysebegriffe zu verfeinern – anhand der queerfeministischen und postkolonialen Theorie zum Beispiel.»

biografischen Anekdoten herausdestillieren. Aber wenn du keinen Weg findest, dort wieder hinauszukommen, ist das nicht toll. Das wollte ich sicher nicht, und hier half mir eine andere Emotion, der Stolz. Man denke an Slogans wie «Gay Pride» oder «Black is beautiful!». Auch Klassenstolz und Widerstand haben miteinander zu tun. Diese beiden Affekte und Haltungen musst du in der Schweizer Geschichte weit, weit suchen gehen. Warum läuft die Auseinandersetzung mit der Illegalisierung der Familien – ein Gesetz, das den Saisonniers von 1934 bis 2002 verboten hatte, ihre Familien nachzuziehen – immer auf diese armen «versteckten Kinder» hinaus? Es ist eine fast unsagbare Wahrheit, dass das Widerstand war und dass diese Familien stolz sein könnten, einfach nicht das gemacht zu haben, was in diesem Gesetz gestanden hat. Die Sprache geht einfach nicht dorthin, zu dieser Wahrheit. Es gibt weisse, blinde Flecken in der Sprachlandschaft.

FP: Weil einem die Sprache fehlt, um die richtigen Fragen zu stellen?

PDM: Auch, ja. Bei einem «Circuit» über Archive in Zürich waren wir vom Schwarzenbach-Komplex beteiligt. Wir haben die Teilnehmenden an den Ort geführt, wo viele illegalisierte Familien lebten, die ich kannte, deren Kinder bei meiner Mutter am Küchentisch gelernt haben. Da haben wir genau das thematisiert, was Du ansprichst, die Ausschreibung lautete: «Wenn die Unwissenden nicht richtig fragen, erhalten sie von den Wissenden Antworten, die vom Gegenstand ablenken – und wenn die Wissenden nicht richtig antworten, wird man nie wissen, wie man richtig fragt.» Wobei ich heute sagen würde, es geht nicht so sehr um das Nicht-wissen-Können, als um das Nicht-verstehen-Wollen.

FP: Da kommt mir die Führung von Living Library im Rahmen der Ausstellung im Neuen Museum Biel/Bienne «Wir, die Saisonniers … 1931–2022» in den Sinn, an der wir beide teilgenommen haben. Dort haben ehemalige Saisonniers und Saisonnières und auch deren Nachkommen ihre Geschichte an

theatre. There's an endless supply of material to work on. Only now are we starting to discover Switzerland's colonial past, and this also has a gender aspect, which in turn has a past and present within the history of class. Why leave Switzerland out?

FP: Is it due to the cliché that everyone in Switzerland is "rich"?

PDM: Probably. I think it's also become a cliché to say that Switzerland emerged from the Second World War unscathed. Who paid the price for that? A lot of things have been swept under the carpet, like the brutal way indentured child labourers, Jenisch, Sinti and Roma families were treated until well into the 1970s, the Jewish refugees who were turned back at the border and the unscrupulous art dealers who profited from their property – indeed, the whole discourse on immigration spiralling out of control. Someone had to pay for the ones who got off scot-free – not least Switzerland's women, who waited so long for political integration.

FP: Perception of these contexts and history is linked to language, isn't it? Ivna Žic addresses this issue in her book *Wahrscheinliche Herkünfte*. She suggests that we should ask each other new questions instead of "Where do you come from?"

PDM: Yes, I basically agree with that, although the question has a different subtext when you think of *social* origin, doesn't it? It's extremely productive to ask which class someone is from. I do it regularly in my seminars.

I don't know if it's about language as such or more about reflection on linguistic resources, asking yourself what you need language for. Where is the collective denial of class issues so strong in this country that I'm not even allowed to say certain things out loud? I'm often confronted with a deep-rooted hostility towards the intellectual that acts like a brick wall. I think that's a key blind spot. We certainly have people who are linguistically gifted. We have a literary elite, they just steer clear of certain topics. I felt the need to go for the low-hanging fruit, have a lick and then describe how it tastes. I found writing about that highly satisfying. It was also interesting to note quite routinely over time that Bourdieu is all well and good, but his arguments have their limits. I wanted to go further and refine the analytical vocabulary – based on queer-feminist and postcolonial theory, for example.

B.   Photo from the *Circuit* event

FP: Which analytical vocabulary do you mean?

PDM: I noticed that cultural sociology has a tendency to become fixated on experiences of shame. The term "pride" doesn't even feature in the sociological lexicon, but there are very extensive definitions of "shame" and "guilt". I found Annie Ernaux's assertion very important. She said that social details become clearly discernible in shame and humiliation. Shame is thus a sort of personal medium for investigating social structures of inequality, taking you straight to the point where theory and practice meet. In terms of collective history with a capital H, we can derive a great deal of value from these biographical anecdotes, but it isn't good to get stuck in that rut. I wanted to avoid that, and it was another emotion that helped me: pride. Think of such slogans as "gay pride" or "black is beautiful". Class pride and resistance are also linked, although you need to search long and hard to find them in Swiss history. Why does any account of the outlawing of families by the legislation on seasonal workers, which forbade them from bringing their families along from 1934 to 2002, always centre on the poor, "hidden" children? It's an almost unspeakable truth that this was a form of resistance, that these families could take pride in not having followed the letter of the law. Language simply doesn't go there. It has blind spots.

FP: Because we don't have the language to ask the right questions?

PDM: That too, yes. I took part in a Circuit event on archives in Zurich with the Schwarzenbach-Komplex collective, and we took people to a place where lots of these illegalised families lived. I knew them, and their children would have lessons with my mother at the kitchen table. We discussed the very topic you just touched on. It was described thus: "If those who do not know do not

"I wanted to go further and refine the analytical vocabulary – based on queer-feminist and postcolonial theory, for example."

ask the right questions, they will receive misleading answers from those who do know. If those who know do not give the right answers, one can never know how to ask the right questions." These days, I'd say that it's less about not knowing and more about not wanting to understand.

FP: That reminds me of the Living Library tour we both took part in that accompanied the Neues Museum Biel exhibition *Wir, die Saisonniers … 1931–2022*[4]. Former seasonal workers and their descendants told their stories at historically significant locations around the city. One lady stood outside the Congress House and told of her uncle, who had an emotional connection to the building as he had worked on its construction.

PDM: I also wrote about that subject, in Italian for the first time so my mother could understand it! In *Cara Mamma*, I describe exactly what that lady was talking about. My parents moved back to Italy when they retired, and my father would sometimes disappear all of a sudden when they came

historischen Schauplätzen in der Stadt erzählt. Eine Frau hat vor dem Kongressgebäude über ihren Onkel erzählt, der eine emotionale Bindung zum Gebäude verspürte, an dem er mitgebaut hatte.

PDM: Zu dem Thema habe ich auch geschrieben, zum ersten Mal auf Italienisch, damit es auch meine Mutter versteht! Ich beschreibe in «Cara Mamma» genau das, was diese Frau auch sagt. Wenn meine Eltern, die seit ihrer Pensionierung in Italien lebten, mich in der Schweiz besuchten, verschwand ab und zu mein Vater, ganz plötzlich. Er besuche alle «seine» ehemaligen Baustellen, um zu schauen, wie der Zustand «seiner» Häuser ist. Er nahm mich dann auch einmal auf den Rundgang mit. Zwei Sachen sind mir dabei aufgefallen. Das Erste: Er hat seine Häuser immer so zärtlich getätschelt, wie ein Freund einen alten Kumpel. Und das Zweite: Er nannte nie eine Jahreszahl, wenn ich ihn danach fragte, wann das Gebäude gebaut worden war, sondern er sagte zum Beispiel: «Da bist Du gerade in den Kindergarten gekommen.» Oder: «Da hast Du die Prüfung bestanden, um Textildesign zu studieren.» Die Stadt war sein Maurermeter mit der Chronologie meines Werdegangs. Seine Kinder waren Sinn und Zweck seines Arbeiterlebens. Seither sehe ich die Stadt mit komplett anderen Augen. Ich bin voller Dankbarkeit dafür.

FP: Du hast dadurch einen ganz neuen Blick auf Deine Biografie erhalten.

PDM: Genau. Meine Biografie ist eingeschrieben in den Häusern dieser Stadt. In Parkhäusern, in Banken, in Versicherungen, in Schulen. Im gleichen Artikel schreibe ich auch über meine Mutter: «Du hast mich wahrscheinlich auch immer mitgenommen, beim Putzen. Übrigens nehme ich dich auch immer mit, denn ich erzähle ja immer von dir.» Wir wurden als Saisonnierfamilie unter Zwang auseinandergerissen. Diese Verbindungen durch Erzählungen wieder herzustellen, ist sehr wichtig für den Heilungsprozess des historischen Traumas, das das Saisonnierstatut hinterlassen hat.

FP: Du bedienst ganz viele Ausdrucksformate, Blogs, offene Briefe, Interviews, eine Dissertation, ein Hörspiel, Performances usw., mit denen Du je nach Format unterschiedlich auf ein Thema hinweisen kannst. Wie schaffst Du es, im Gleichgewicht zu bleiben?

PDM: Das fordert mich sehr, das ist etwas Anstrengendes. Am krassesten habe ich es erlebt mit dem offenen Brief «Brennende Unschärfe» an Simonetta Sommaruga für die INES-Webseite.[4] Ich sollte den Brieftext vor Publikum am Theaterspektakel in Zürich performen. Ich habe aber gemerkt,

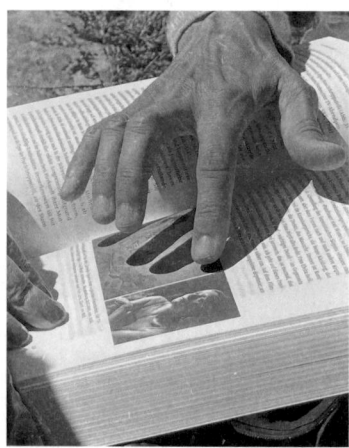

C. Paola De Martin, *Cara Mamma*, in: *trans magazin*: journal of the Department of Architecture, ETH Zurich, No. 42, 2023, pp. 146–151

«Ja, das Kollektiv aufzubauen ist ein schönes Gefühl! Ein Versuch, meine Geborgenheit in der Grossfamilie in Italien in der Schweiz wiederherzustellen?»

dass ich das nicht einfach so vorlesen kann! Zentral war die Frage: Wie kann ich den Inhalt dieses Briefs performen, ohne in ein emotionales Loch hineinzufallen? Es war unabdingbar, eine Transformation des geschriebenen Textes für die Bühne zu erarbeiten. Das war für mich eine unglaubliche Erkenntnis. In jedem Medium muss man das Gleichgewicht eines an sich vertrauten Themas für sich wieder neu finden.

FP: Bei Deiner Arbeit gehst Du von Deinen individuellen Erfahrungen aus, benennst Sachverhalte und involvierst andere Menschen. Der Verein TESORO basiert auf individuellen Geschichten und wird dann durch den Austausch zu einer kollektiven Erfahrung.

PDM: Ja, das Kollektiv aufzubauen ist ein schönes Gefühl! Ein Versuch, meine Geborgenheit in der Grossfamilie in Italien in der Schweiz wiederherzustellen? Als wir den Verein TESORO gegründet haben, hat sich Philip Ursprung, mein Doktorvater, überraschend bei mir gemeldet, um anlässlich der Gründung etwas zu sagen. Unter anderem erwähnte er, dass es aus der Logik von *Give us a break!* völlig klar sei, dass dieser Verein zeitgleich, also 2021, gegründet werde.[5] Mein Doktorat folgt nicht nur einer individuellen Logik und der verborgenen Logik des Designfeldes, sondern mich hat die Illegalisierung von Saisonnierfamilien während der Arbeit an diesem Buch plötzlich auch sehr viel mehr zu interessieren begonnen.

FP: Wie kam das?

PDM: Als ich schon ziemlich weit mit dem Schreiben war, stiess ich auf den Modernismus, auf die Avantgarden der Zwischenkriegszeit und ihre Verstrickungen mit der eugenisch motivierten Rassenhygiene. Dabei stellte ich fest, dass meine Erfahrung nicht beschränkt werden kann auf die «Arbeiterkind-wird-Designerin-Erfahrung» der zweiten Hälfte des 20. Jahrhunderts, sondern sie weist zurück auf das ANAG (*Bundesgesetz von 1931 über Aufenthalt und Niederlassung der Ausländer*) – die Zwischenkriegszeit also. Aus dem Zusammenhang heraus ergeben sich jetzt die Fragen: Was war da eigentlich los in diesem Land? Was ist in einer gesellschaftlichen «Grenzbereinigung» – so drücken sich die Väter des ANAG aus – die Rolle der modernistischen Ästhetik? Wo waren denn die Design-, Architektur-, Literaturschaffenden – die sich gegen das ANAG gewehrt hätten?

FP: Das ist ja auch etwas, wo Du aktuell daran arbeitest, oder?

PDM: Ja, denn das *ist* immer noch aktuell. Es ist nicht so, dass wir moralisch über der Vergangenheit stünden. Das ist Nonsens. Darum interessiert mich der Widerstand so sehr; denn ich glaube, dass es diesen immer gegeben hat, aber er wurde systematisch aus dem kollektiven Gedächtnis gelöscht.

to visit me in Switzerland. He was visiting all of "his" old construction sites to see what condition "his" buildings were in. He once took me on the tour. Two things struck me. Firstly, he always stroked the buildings so gently, like he was touching an old friend. Secondly, when I asked when a particular building was built, he wouldn't say a year, he'd say something like "You'd just started kindergarten" or "You'd just passed your exam to get on the textile design course." The whole city was his timeline of my life. His children were what gave his work meaning and purpose. Ever since then, I've seen the city with completely different eyes. I'm really thankful for that.

FP: It gave you an entirely new perspective on your biography.

PDM: Exactly. My biography is written in the houses of this city, its car parks, banks, insurance companies, schools. In the same article, I also write about my mother: "You probably always took me with you when you were cleaning. I always take you with me too, because I'm always talking about you." As a seasonal worker family, we were forced apart. Reestablishing these links by telling stories is a very important part of the healing process for the historical trauma the law on seasonal workers left behind.

FP: You employ lots of different means of expression: blogs, open letters, interviews, a dissertation, a radio play, performances and so on, allowing you to approach a topic from different angles. How do you manage to strike a balance?

"Yes, building the collective is a great feeling – an attempt, perhaps, to recreate in Switzerland the feeling of belonging I get from my extended family in Italy?"

PDM: It's very hard work. It was hardest of all when I wrote the open letter *Brennende Unschärfe* to Federal Councillor Simonetta Sommaruga for the INES website.[5] I was to hold a spoken-word performance in front of an audience at the Zürcher Theaterspektakel, but I realised that I couldn't just read the letter straight from the page. The key question was how to perform its content without falling into an emotional hole. I needed to adapt the letter for the stage. That was quite a revelation for me. However familiar the material, you have to strike the right balance anew for each medium.

FP: Your work is based on your own experiences, but it also focuses on facts and involves other people. The association TESORO was founded on individual stories coming together to create a collective experience.

PDM: Yes, building the collective is a great feeling – an attempt, perhaps, to recreate in Switzerland the feeling of belonging I get from my extended family in Italy? When we founded TESORO, my PhD supervisor Philip Ursprung contacted me out of the blue, and one of the things he said was that starting the association right away (in 2021) was an obvious logical progression from *Give us a break!*[6] My doctorate not only follows an individual logic and the hidden logic of the design field, working on it also caused me suddenly to take a much greater interest in the illegalisation of seasonal worker families.

FP: How did that manifest itself?

PDM: I was already quite far along with the writing when I came across Modernism, the inter-war avant-gardes and their intermingling with eugenically motivated racial hygiene. I realised that my experience can't be reduced to the single story of "working-class girl makes it as a designer" in the second half of the 20th century but instead harks back to the Federal Act of 1931 on the Temporary and Permanent Residence of Foreign Nationals, i.e. the period between the two World Wars. This raised new questions: What on earth was going on in this country? What is the role of Modernist aesthetics in an "adjustment of social boundaries", as the authors of this law called it? And where were the designers, architects, writers who opposed the law?

FP: That's something you're working on at the moment, isn't it?

PDM: Yes, because it's *still* an issue. It's not like we're morally superior to those who came before us. That's nonsense. That's why I'm so interested in resistance. I think it has always existed but been systematically erased from the collective memory. There have always been people who didn't accept this strange "adjustment", they just didn't have a voice that's explicitly expressed in any of the literature on design history.

FP: Are there in fact any physical sources, or has it tended to be passed down through word of mouth?

PDM: It's amazing how many sources you can actually find in the archives, and the dogma of racial hygiene was not covered up at all before the Second World War. It was after the War, however, and much was euphemised in light of the Holocaust. Knowledge of it became highly coded, hidden away and symptomatically passed down from generation to generation of those affected by the law and other forms of state coercion. That's why you're so important as well, Francesca. You're the next generation, so to speak, still interested in what happened to your mother, your grandmother and so many other families who were split up. Some great concepts have been developed, such as Saidiya Hartman's "critical fabulation". She has very cleverly and methodically used speculation as a means of shedding light on

D. TESORO business card.
Illustration © Nando von Arb

Es gab schon immer Leute, die diese seltsame «Säuberung» abwegig gefunden haben. Die hatten einfach keine Stimme, die in den Quellen des Kanons der Designgeschichte explizit wird.

FP: Gibt es Quellen, die physisch vorhanden sind, oder handelt es sich auch oftmals um Narrationen, die mündlich weitergegeben wurden?

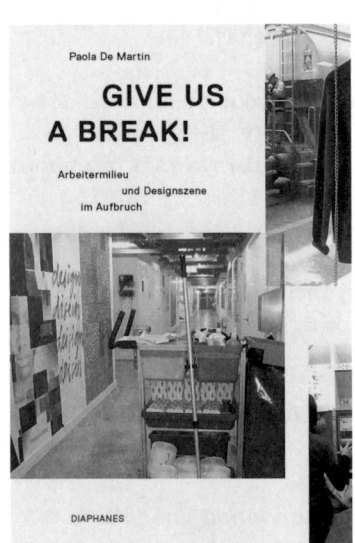

E. Cover of *Give us a Break! Arbeitermilieu und Designszene im Aufbruch*, Diaphanes

PDM: Es ist erstaunlich, wie viele Quellen man tatsächlich in den Archiven finden kann, und bis zum Zweiten Weltkrieg wurden die rassenhygienischen Dogmen überhaupt nicht verheimlicht. Danach hingegen schon, unter dem Vorzeichen der Katastrophe der Shoah wurde viel euphemisiert. Danach wurde das Wissen darüber sehr codiert, verklausuliert und symptomatisch von Generation zu Generation der Betroffenen vom ANAG und anderen staatlichen Zwangsmassnahmen weitergegeben. Darum bist Du, Francesca, auch so wichtig. Du bist quasi die nächste Generation, die es immer noch interessiert, was mit Deiner Grossmutter und Mutter, was mit den vielen Familien passiert ist, die getrennt wurden. Es gibt mittlerweile tolle Konzepte, wie Saidiya Hartmans «critical fabulation». Hartman hat das Spekulieren methodisch sehr klug als Potential für die Forschung von blinden Flecken genutzt. Eine leidenschaftliche, geduldige Arbeit, *santa pazienza*, wie man auf Italienisch sagt!

FP: Du sammelst Zitate mit diskriminierenden Aussagen, Stereotypen und klischeehaften Vorstellungen.

PDM: Ich sammle eigentlich Indizien. Viele Menschen, die über Diskriminierung nachdenken, wissen gar nicht, wo anfangen mit der Aufarbeitung, die Hinweise sind schlicht überwältigend. Mein Tipp ist dann jeweils: Bündle Indizien und sortiere sie in Kisten mit allem, was dort hineingehört. Irgendwann hat man viel Material beisammen. Mit der Zeit kristallisieren sich die Schwerpunkte heraus, um darüber nachzudenken: Was sind die Ähnlichkeiten? Was sind die Unterschiede? Wo gibt es Leitmotive? Ich sehe das Sammeln auch als eine Form des Widerstands.

FP: Können wir hier nochmals zu TESORO übergehen? Wie hängt der Verein mit Deiner Arbeit als Designforscherin zusammen?

PDM: Was mich in diesem Zusammenhang stark beschäftigt, ist der Konsumrassismus, bezogen auf die Italiener:innen in der Schweiz. Ab etwa Anfang 1980er-Jahre war alles toll, was vorher verachtet

«Die Gentrifizierung der Köpfe erfolgte vor der Gentrifizierung der Stadtquartiere.»

wurde. Zum Beispiel die Mode, das Essen, also die sogenannte *Italianità*. Alles daran wurde glattpoliert und entkoppelt von einer sehr gewaltvollen vergangenen Realität. Man nimmt nur etwas, was einem passt, und den Rest will man dann nicht wissen und verdrängt es total. Begriffe wie «Lieblings-Migranten», «Parade-Ausländer», oder «Integrations-Heroes» mögen das verdeutlichen. Das hat mich wirklich sauer gemacht.

FP: Du hast diese Instrumentalisierung viel bewusster mitbekommen als ich.

F. Christina Cogdell, *Eugenic Design. Streamlining America in the 1930s*, Philadelphia, University of Pennsylvania Press, 2010

PDM: Eine Zumutung war das, weisst Du! Auch als ich an der Kunstgewerbeschule war, hiess es: «Ah, Italien. Milano, die Möbelmesse, Florenz, Textilmesse, Prada, Gucci, Tiramisù und Rucola. Alles toll, alles gut.» Das Verachtete wurde zum «Schrägen» und dann wurde es «in». Die Arbeiterquartiere und die Industriegelände, in denen wir lebten und arbeiteten, sowie unsere Freizeit, das Fussballschauen oder die Schrebergärten zum Beispiel, waren plötzlich hipp. Die Gentrifizierung der Köpfe erfolgte vor der Gentrifizierung der Stadtquartiere.

FP: Diese Wut darüber ist immer noch da. Ich, eine Generation nach Dir, ich bin immer noch wütend. Einerseits über die Ungerechtigkeiten in der Gesellschaft, aber auch über das Unausgesprochene in der eigenen Familie.

PDM: Widersprüchlich, nicht? Im Schweigen ist viel Wissen gespeichert! Irgendwann habe ich festgestellt, dass ich mit meiner Familie genau durch den Stau von Energie, die nicht fliessen durfte, verbunden bin. Mit dem Ende der Doktorarbeit habe ich gemerkt, dass der Stau weg ist. Heute spüre ich eine fliessende Verbundenheit. Wenn ich jetzt etwas mache, dann nehme ich Energie von anderen, aber ich gebe sie gleich wieder weiter und hoffe auch, dass das, was ich tue, für andere zum Vermächtnis wird. Dass das Buch gelesen und gebraucht wird.

FP: Was mich auch umtreibt, ist das Publikum bei meinen Lesungen oder Vorträgen. Was kommt bei den Leuten überhaupt an?

PDM: Da kommt mir Louise Bourgeois in den Sinn, die gesagt hat: Man muss sich ständig wiederholen, sonst verstehen die Leute nicht, was man sagen will. Sprachliche Wiederholungen sind eine Analogie zu visuellen Mustern. Man muss es nochmals und nochmals sagen. Und dabei versuchen, gemeinsam mit dem Publikum vom Wissen, dass Dinge geschehen sind, zum

G. Teju Cole, *Blind Spots*, London: Faber & Faber, 2017

the blind spots. It's a passionate and patient endeavour – *santa pazienza*, as we say in Italian!

FP: You collect quotations that contain discriminatory statements, stereotyping and clichés.

PDM: What I'm really collecting is evidence. A lot of people who want to study discrimination don't know where to start, there's just so much to deal with. My tip is to gather evidence and sort it into related boxes. Before you know it, you'll have plenty of material. Then you'll eventually start to understand what you need to focus on: What are the similarities? What are the differences? Are there any overriding themes? I see this act of collecting as a form of resistance too.

FP: Can we go back to TESORO at this point? How does it relate to your work as a design researcher?

PDM: In this respect, I'm very much concerned with consumer racism in relation to Italians in Switzerland. From about the early 1980s onwards, everything that had previously been reviled was suddenly cool: the fashions, the food, *italianità* in general. It was all polished up and completely decoupled from the very violent reality of the past. People just take what they like and ignore the rest. Terms like "favourite immigrant", "model foreigner" and "integration heroes" only underscore that. That has made me really angry.

FP: You experienced this instrumentalisation much more consciously than I have.

PDM: It was insulting, you know? Even at art school, people would say, "Ah, Italy. Milan, the furniture fair, Florence, the textile fair, Prada, Gucci, tiramisu and rocket. It's all so lovely." What was once scorned became "offbeat" and then "in". The working-class neighbourhoods and factories where we lived and worked, our hobbies like watching football and tending our allotments, these things were suddenly fashionable. Gentrification happened in people's minds before it became visible on the streets.

"Gentrification happened in people's minds before it became visible on the streets."

FP: This anger is still present. I'm a generation younger than you, and yet I'm angry too – not only about social injustice, but also about the things left unsaid in my own family.

PDM: It's a contradiction, isn't it? There's a lot of knowledge locked up in that silence. There came a point where I realised it's precisely that pent-up energy that binds me to my family. When I completed my dissertation, it felt like that energy had finally been released. Now the connection flows through me. When I do something, I draw energy from others, but I also pass it on, and I hope that others get something out of what I do. I hope that people read the book and benefit from it.

FP: Something that preoccupies me is the audience when I give a reading or a lecture. Is anything I say really getting through to them?

PDM: That brings to mind Louise Bourgeois, who said that you have to repeat yourself constantly if you want people to understand what you're trying to say. Saying the same thing over and over again is analogous to a visual pattern. You have to take your audience on a journey from knowing what happened to understanding how it could happen.

FP: You refer to the healing effect of repetition as your "three-part harmony": "I really exist!", "It's not my fault that I exist!", "My existence has been worthwhile!"

PDM: Yes, perception, recognition and language are inextricably linked. Being born in this country, where the family you're born into isn't allowed to exist, naturally resonates for the rest of your life, but it was precisely this trauma that led me to the conclusion I drew in my dissertation: Modernism, racial hygiene and migration are closely tied together. What seemed like "my" problem turned out to be a very healthy instinct. I learned not to stop working on a guided, speculative fantasy when the alarm bells started ringing. It was in this context that I discovered the term "eugenic design". This catastrophic connection can be found anywhere in the world where there is a strong leaning towards modern progress – apart from Switzerland. I'm challenging this image of innocent Switzerland with a new hypothesis. Either Swiss architecture, art and design were a hotbed of resistance against racial hygiene and eugenics, or we have a huge blind spot. Both are probably true, but they definitely can't both be false. We should research the subject, overcome the lack of language and dare to take a leap into the unknown.

H. Patricia Purtschert, *Kolonialität und Geschlecht im 20. Jahrhundert. Eine Geschichte der weissen Schweiz*, Transcript, 2019

FP: One way you have overcome this lack of language is by reading countless books over the years. What are your favourites?

PDM: I particularly loved three books that gave me courage on occasions when I would get scared by what I found out. I wouldn't be where I am today without them. *King Kong Theory* by Virginie Despentes showed me that you can recover from traumatic experiences if you have the resources

Verstehen, wie sie geschehen konnten, zu gelangen.

FP: Den heilsamen Effekt des Wiederholens nennst Du auch Deinen «Dreiklang»: «Es gibt mich, tatsächlich!», «Ich bin nicht Schuld, dass es mich gibt!», «Dafür war es wert, zu leben!».

PDM: Ja, Wahrnehmung, Anerkennung und Sprache sind existenziell verbunden. Als Kind hierzulande auf die Welt zu kommen, wo es die Familie, in die man geboren wurde, nicht geben darf, natürlich macht das einen Resonanzraum auf fürs ganze Leben. Aber genau die traumatische Verletzung hat mich überhaupt erst zu der Erkenntnis meiner Doktorarbeit geführt: Modernismus und Rassenhygiene und Migration sind eng verbunden. Was scheinbar «mein» Problem war, entpuppte sich als ein sehr gesunder Instinkt. Ich habe gelernt, nicht aufzuhören, mit einer geführten, spekulativen Fantasie zu arbeiten, wenn die Alarmglocken läuten. In diesem Zusammenhang bin ich auf den Begriff «eugenisches Design» gestossen. Überall auf dem Globus findet man den verhängnisvollen Zusammenhang, wo es den machtvollen Hang zum modernen Fortschritt gibt – nur in der Schweiz nicht. Ich fordere dieses Bild der Schweiz mit einer neuen Hypothese heraus. Entweder war die Schweizer Architektur-, Kunst- und Designszene ein Ort des Widerstands gegen Rassenhygiene und Eugenik oder wir haben es mit einem massiven blinden Fleck zu tun. Vermutlich stimmen beide Hypothesen, aber sicher ist, es können nicht beide Hypothesen falsch sein. Wir sollten dazu forschen, die Sprachlosigkeit überwinden, und über unsere Schatten springen.

FP: Diese Sprachlosigkeit hast Du über die Jahre hinweg auch mit unzähligen Lektüren überwunden. Was sind Deine liebsten Begleiter?

PDM: Besonders lieb wurden mir drei Bücher, die mir Mut gemacht haben, wenn ich manchmal Angst vor meinen Entdeckungen hatte. Bücher, ohne die ich nicht da wäre, wo ich heute stehe. «King Kong Theorie» von Virginie Despentes, das mir aufgezeigt hat, dass man aus traumatischen Erfahrungen heil herauskommen kann, wenn man die Ressourcen hat (und für die lohnt es sich zu kämpfen!), um den Verlust des eigenen Opferstatuts zu trauern. «Blind Spots» von Teju Cole, das ich unendlich oft lesen und anschauen kann, wobei diese eigensinnigen, heilsamen Fotos und Essays nicht aufhören, mich zu überraschen und zu nähren. Und ganz entscheidend in der Schlussphase meiner Dissertation war «Kolonialität und Geschlecht. Eine Geschichte der weissen Schweiz» von Patricia Purtschert. Das Buch hat meine These enorm gestützt, dass die «Modernisierung» des Wohnens, der Küche und des Haushalts in der Zwischenkriegszeit auch in der Schweiz ein verführerischer Backlash gegen die Emanzipation der Frauen gewesen ist, die wiederum eng mit der Kolonialgeschichte und der Geschichte der Sklaverei verstrickt ist.

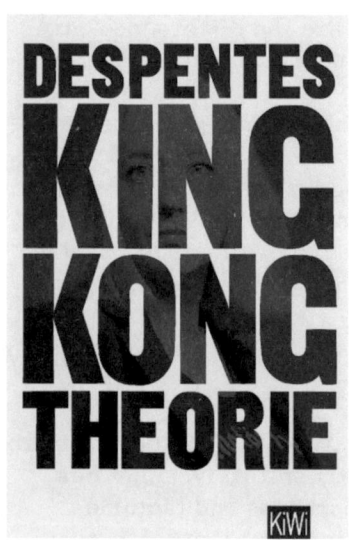

I. Virginie Despentes, *King Kong Theorie*, Köln: Kiepenheuer & Witsch, 2010

1. Vgl. SRF2 Kultur, Künste im Gespräch, Noëmi Gradwohl: «Soziale Herkunft und Design – Paola De Martins Recherche», 2.3.2023.
2. Paola De Martin: «Cara Mamma», in: *trans magazin*: journal of the Department of Architecture, ETH Zurich, No. 42, 2023, pp. 146–151.
3. Ausstellung im Neuen Museum Biel, «Wir, die Saisonniers… 1931 – 2022», 17.12.2022 – 25.6.2023.
4. Paola De Martin: «Brennende Unschärfe», in: INES (Hg.), Zürich: Diaphanes, 2021, S.27–33.
5. Vgl. SRF Kultur, Kontext: «Saisonnierstatut: Das war ein Attentat auf die Familien», 07.12.2021.

(and it's worth fighting for them!) to grieve the loss of your own victim status. *Blind Spot* by Teju Cole is one I can endlessly re-read and pore over. His idiosyncratic, healing photos and essays never cease to surprise and comfort me. One book that was vital while I was finishing my dissertation was *Kolonialität und Geschlecht. Eine Geschichte der weissen Schweiz* by Patricia Purtschert. It lent huge support to my theory that, in Switzerland too, the "modernisation" of living, cooking and housekeeping between the wars was a seductive backlash against the emancipation of women, which in turn is tightly intertwined with the history of colonialism and slavery.

1. See SRF2 Kultur, Künste im Gespräch, Noëmi Gradwohl: *Soziale Herkunft und Design – Paola De Martins Recherche*, 2 March 2023.
2. Paola De Martin, *Cara Mamma*, in: *trans magazin*: journal of the Department of Architecture, ETH Zurich, No. 42, 2023, pp. 146–151.
3. In the German-speaking part of Switzerland in 1900, Carl Alfred Schmid coined the specific term "Überfremdung", which has since become very popular. It literally translates as "over-foreignisation".
4. Exhibition at the Neues Museum Biel, *Wir, die Saisonniers… 1931–2022*, 17 December 2022–25 June 2023.
5. Paola De Martin, *Brennende Unschärfe*, in: INES (ed.), Zurich, Diaphanes, 2021, pp. 27–33.
6. See SRF Kultur, Kontext: *Saisonnierstatut: Das war ein Attentat auf die Familien*, 7 December 2021.

materielle Arbeit
immaterielle Unruhe
putzen
kochen
aufkochen
aufbrezeln
ausfressen
nicht vergessen
auf- und abbauen
geniessen
anlehnen
ablehnen
spicken
spucken
fluchen
spinnen
singen
genau ticken
anders takten
umschreiben
umwerben
bewerben
immateriell arbeiten
materiell ruhen

material labour
immaterial restlessness
clean
cook
boil up
dress up
ring wrong
never forget
assemble and disassemble
enjoy
align with
reject
cheat
spit
swear
spin
sing
tick exactly
clock differently
rewrite
woo woo
apply for
work immaterially
rest materially

Translated from the German original

Vengo anch'io,
no tu no
Non ti fidar di me se il
cuor ti manca
Chi non risica
non rosica
Cara mamma
O volere o volare
Lo sai che
i papaveri son alti
alti alti

I'll come too,
no not you
Don't trust me if you
lack courage
Nothing ventured,
nothing gained
Dear Mama
To want or to fly
You know that
poppies are tall
tall tall

Translated from the Italian original

Long-time companions:
James Baldwin
Ruth Klüger
Giorgio Gaber
Emma Kunz

Paola De Martin
Avanti guanti: la nuova avanguardia è pronta!

di Francesca Petrarca

Ho visto Paola in foto prima ancora di sapere chi fosse. Ho letto i suoi blog prima ancora di sapere come parlasse. Quando ho sentito la sua voce alla radio, le sue parole mi hanno conquistata[1]. Paola De Martin ha la capacità di smuovere: se stessa, me e gli altri. È una «studiosa attivista». Il suo percorso è un modello unico nel suo genere, il suo lavoro una ricerca sul design che indaga le connessioni nascoste tra estetica, società e classe. In numerose pubblicazioni ha detto addio al silenzio. Nelle azioni pacifiche trova la giusta espressione per la sua protesta. Ai contesti sociali carichi di tensione dei nostri tempi contrappone un disarmo simbolico. Sempre curiosa, mai sola.

L'attività di Paola è come un lavoro a maglia: intreccia letteratura, arte e design, unisce storia, sociologia e creazione visiva, e si rivolge agli altri. È una metamorfosi che assorbe diversi elementi e da cui nascono oggetti, performance, lezioni, lettere, foto, musica, radiodrammi, saggi e articoli. Nella sua attività di insegnamento presso le scuole universitarie di design e come post dottoranda al Politecnico federale di Zurigo, Paola attrae molti studenti e studentesse. Insegna loro a riflettere sull'esclusione e li incoraggia a confrontarsi in modo intersezionale con l'estrazione sociale e i privilegi. Docente «d'impatto», porta avanti una riflessione sulle norme, le regole e le strutture che offre ad altri nuove vie da percorrere. Pone accenti critici e trasmette impulsi alle giovani generazioni di designer. Nel suo lavoro l'espressione orale nutre la riflessione scritta e viceversa. Grazie alla collaborazione con il collettivo Schwarzenbach-Komplex, la «solitudine della maratoneta» si è trasformata in una rete di amicizie. L'associazione TESORO, da lei fondata, risponde al grande interesse del pubblico per la rivisitazione critica della politica familiare svizzera. Nelle mani di Paola i temi sociali sono come fili magici che a ogni punto della maglia creano un nuovo intreccio.

Se per le prime femministe la sfera privata era politica, per Paola la domanda fondamentale è: «Quanto è politica l'estetica»? Mi ha regalato un paio guanti fatti a mano con un complesso motivo in verde e rosa. Lavorando a maglia riesce a organizzare i pensieri e a ricaricarsi di forza interiore mentre fuori il mondo è freddo e cinico. La resistenza costruttiva è profondamente radicata in lei. Tra i suoi ricordi d'infanzia vi è una maestra di maglia e cucito della scuola elementare di Zurigo-Affoltern che le proibiva di lavorare a maglia alla maniera «italiana», perché era diversa dalla sua. Inoltre, se avesse fatto un errore «italiano», non avrebbe potuto aiutarla. Fortunatamente, Paola ha combinato le due tecniche, inizialmente di nascosto, e in seguito ha fatto della combinazione il suo leitmotiv.

Nella tesi di dottorato «Give us a break! Arbeitermilieu und Designszene im Aufbruch» (Diaphanes, 2020), incentrata sugli ambienti operai e sulla scena del design, a poco a poco la lingua di Paola si srotola come un tappeto definendo un linguaggio che crea lo spazio per raccontare storie fino a quel momento inascoltate. Paola si confronta con il sentimento di appartenenza e non appartenenza al mondo del design zurighese in cui si trova immersa negli anni Novanta, prima come studentessa di design tessile e poi come cofondatrice del marchio di moda Beige. Il suo punto di partenza sono le esperienze vissute in ragione della sua estrazione sociale, come figlia di una famiglia operaia immigrata e di bassa istruzione scolastica. Alla fine riesce a individuare quelle distorsioni storiche del design che un tempo la disorientavano. Osserva con esattezza il non detto, grande quanto un elefante eppure ignorato dagli «eredi del capitale culturale». Come ricercatrice espone sé stessa indagando con spirito di autoriflessione il tessuto in cui è inserita, le discriminazioni subite e i privilegi ricevuti. Paola attinge sia alla teoria che alla letteratura autobiografica e intreccia il tutto in una fitta trama di relazioni. La sua tesi fa luce sul sistema in cui noi designer siamo inseriti. È una critica manifesta alle strutture esistenti che escludono ed etichettano automaticamente le persone provenienti da classi svantaggiate, mentre ne privilegiano e ne favoriscono altre.

Le strofe di questo manifesto sono come i fili colorati dei miei guanti. La protesta nel continuare a fare a maglia a modo suo nonostante la maestra le imponesse di fare «come si deve», la protesta dei genitori nel riportare la piccola Paola in Svizzera nonostante l'ordine di espulsione della polizia degli stranieri, la protesta del non rimanere più in silenzio, il pugno che si apre piano piano nella lotta per la giustizia: tutto inizia con un punto «sbagliato», che

---

1. Fonti: Mali Lazell, Julia Haenni: ICH WILL ALLES! Streikporträts, edition clandestin 2021, s.p.; «Brennende Unschärfe – Offener Brief an Bundesrätin Simonetta Sommaruga», Istituto Nuova Svizzera INES, Blog, 21.9.2018; «Per arrivare bisogna partire», Istituto Nuova Svizzera INES, Blog, 4.11.2019; «Saisonnierstatut: Das war ein Attentat auf die Familien» (SRF 2 Kultur, « Kontext », 7.12.2021).

diventa un guanto ribelle in cerca di un suo pari. I nostri ricordi vanno avanti mano nella mano: una volta mia nonna mi ha mostrato i raffinati guanti all'uncinetto che indossava per le passeggiate in Italia e poi in Svizzera. Purtroppo sono andati persi, e questa perdita pesa più di quanto si possa pensare. Fa riecheggiare quel senso di perdita tramandato da mia nonna, che in Svizzera non ha potuto vivere con la propria figlia, mia madre. I guanti di Paola cominciano ora a sanare questa ferita. Le mie mani «lavorate a maglia» diventano un canto magico, le file di punti un ammaliante ritornello. Questo ritmo fatato libera energia come un fiume che scorre.

Non è un caso che una designer «arricchita dall'esperienza migratoria» si chieda: «Quanto è politica l'estetica»? Paola apre uno spazio di riflessione che prima non c'era, invitandoci a riflettere sul classismo e su altre forme di discriminazione nella nostra cultura. Fa un passo coraggioso dall'«io» al «noi» quando sottolinea che «non possiamo scegliere la classe in cui nasciamo, ma possiamo capire, comunicare e, se vogliamo, anche cambiare i giudizi e i riflessi estetici che nascono da questa casualità». *Avanti guanti*: la nuova avanguardia è pronta!

Francesca Petrarca ha studiato storia dell'arte, scienze dei media, comunicazione visiva e scienze dell'immagine a Basilea e lavora come designer di libri indipendente. Il suo libro No grazie, non fumo, *è un ritratto letterario e grafico della storia migratoria della nonna dell'autrice. La seconda edizione è uscita nel 2024 per la casa editrice edition clandestin.*

Paola De Martin

Avanti guanti – the new avant-garde is ready for action!

di Francesca Petrarca

I first encountered Paola in a photo before I knew where she stands. I read her blogs before I knew how she speaks. When I heard her voice on the radio, I was struck by what she has to say.[1] Paola De Martin is a mover. She moves herself, me, and others too. She is a scholar-activist whose career has followed a unique pattern. Her work makes connections. It is activist design research into the unspoken interplay between aesthetics, society, and class. Bidding farewell to silence, she has spoken out in various publications. She excels in peaceful protest, confronting the charged social contexts of the present with symbolic disarmament – always inquisitive, never alone.

There is always this mesh that holds everything together. Encompassing literature, art, and design, her way of working creates links to history and sociology, and is always turned towards others. It is an intertwining metamorphosis that produces objects, performances, lectures, letters, photos, music, radio plays, essays, and articles. In her role as an educator at design schools and as a postdoctoral lecturer at ETH Zurich, Paola is very popular among students. She invites them to reflect on exclusion and encourages them to examine their own social background and privileges from an intersectional perspective. Her thoughtful lectures make an impact, guiding listeners towards new ways of engaging with norms, rules, and structures. She adopts critical standpoints and inspires a new generation of designers. Oral expression fertilises written reflection and vice versa. Her work with the Schwarzenbach-Komplex collective took her from the "loneliness of the long-distance runner" to a close-knit community of like-minded friends. The association she founded, TESORO, has ignited public interest in reassessing Swiss family policy. Paola works her magic on multiple social threads, weaving them into an entirely new fabric.

If the private is political, as the early feminists said, then Paola's central question is this: just how political is *aesthetics*? Paola has gifted me some gloves she knitted herself, featuring a complicated pattern in green and pink. Knitting helps her to organise her thoughts and find inner strength when the outside world is cold and cynical. Constructive resistance is deeply rooted in her. Paola recalls her time at primary school in the Affoltern district of Zurich, where her handicraft teacher told her not to knit "the Italian way" because it was not like the way she taught, and she would not be able to help the

1. Mali Lazell, Julia Haenni: *I want it all! Strike portraits*, edition clandestin 2021, no pagination; *Brennende Unschärfe – Offener Brief an Bundesrätin Simonetta Sommaruga*, Institut Neue Schweiz INES, blog, 21 September 2018; *Per arrivare bisogna partire*, Institut Neue Schweiz INES, blog, 4 November 2019; *Saisonnierstatut: Das war ein Attentat auf die Familien* (SRF 2 Kultur, *Kontext*, 7 December 2021).

young Paola if she made an "Italian mistake". Luckily, Paola was able to combine the two techniques (secretly at first), eventually making the act of combining her leitmotif.

In her dissertation *Give us a break! Arbeitermilieu und Designszene im Aufbruch* (Diaphanes, 2020), Paola's voice unleashes into a distinctive expression that articulates a tapestry of previously untold stories. It deals with feelings of belonging and exclusion on the Zurich design scene that was her workplace in the 1990s as a textile student, and later as co-founder of the fashion label Beige. The starting point is her social background, having experienced limited access to the education system as the child of a migrant working-class family. She ultimately pinpoints the historical inequities in design that had previously caused her a lack of orientation, by carefully examining the unsaid; the elephant in the room ignored by the "inheritors of cultural capital". Unafraid to take risks, Paola exposes herself as a researcher, taking on a reflective approach to her own entanglements, biases, and indeed privileges. She draws on both theory and autobiographical literature to craft a dense web of relations. Her work sheds light on the system within which designers operate. It is a manifest criticism of the established structures that reflexively exclude people with underprivileged backgrounds from the field, pigeonholing them and passing them up by favouring others.

The lines of her manifesto are like the colourful yarns from which my gloves were made. There is protest in carrying on with her knitting, even after the teacher told her to stop and "do it properly". There is protest in her parents bringing her back into Switzerland as a small child, even after the immigration authorities had her deported. There is protest in deciding not to keep quiet anymore. The fist that slowly opens in the fight for justice: it unpicks the flaws in its own fabric and refashions itself into a strong and peerless glove. Our memories go hand in hand. My own *nonna* once showed me the intricate gloves she had crocheted herself, elegant *guanti* that she would don to go out on a stroll in Italy and later Switzerland. Unfortunately, they have gone missing. This loss weighs more heavily than one might think. It echoes in the inherited feeling of my nonna's loss, who was not allowed to live in Switzerland with her own child, my mother. Paola's gloves are starting to heal the wound. The rows of yarn enveloping my hands become an enchanting refrain, a magical rhythm unleashing an energy that flows onwards like a river.

It is hardly a coincidence that a designer with the "advantage" of a migrant background, as she ironically says, should ask the question: just *how* political is aesthetics? Paola opens up an uncharted space for reflection and invites us to think about classism and other forms of discrimination in our culture. She makes a bold transition from "I" to "we" when she states emphatically, "We cannot help which class we are born into, but we can understand and communicate the aesthetic judgements and reflexes to which this quirk of fate gives rise and – if we so choose – even change them." *Avanti guanti* – the new avant-garde is ready for action!

Francesca Petrarca studied art history, media science, visual communication and iconic research in Basel and works as a freelance book designer. The second edition of her book No grazie, non fumo, *a literary and visual account of her grandmother's migration story, is to be published by edition clandestin in 2024.*

[DE → p. 9, FR → p. 10]

Biography

Born in 1965, citizen of Zurich and Belluno (Italy). Lives and works in Zurich.

Education

2013–20 ETH Zurich, Institute for the History and Theory of Architecture (gta Institute), Chair of Prof. P. Ursprung, PhD on completion, nominated for the ETH Zurich Silver Medal for outstanding doctoral theses

2003–11 University of Zurich, General History, History of Art in the Modern Era and History of Economics in combination with Socioeconomics

1992–96 Zurich School of Design (SfGZ), Textile Design course

1985–87 Canton of Zurich training college for primary school teachers

Career

Since 2023 ETH Zurich, gta Institute, postdoctoral researcher under Chair of Prof. P. Ursprung

Since 2022 Schwarzenbach-Komplex. Co-curator and performer of the long-term, collective ethnographic-artistic project for an alternative history of racism and resistance in Switzerland

Since 2021 TESORO. Founder and President of the association for dealing with the suffering of illegalised migrant worker families with seasonal status A and annual residence status B

2010–23 Zurich University of the Arts (ZHdK), Design Department and Cultural Analysis Department, lecturing work focusing on design history and design sociology, interculturality and aesthetics of inequality

2010–16 Lucerne University of Applied Sciences and Arts, Lucerne School of Design, Film and Art, Theory Department and study programme in Textile Design; teaching work and establishing sustainability and design history as focus areas

2012–15 ETH Zurich, gta Institute. Research Assistant under Chair of Prof. P. Ursprung

2009–10 University of Zurich, University Research Priority Program (URPP) Asia and Europe, assistant to Prof. S. Trakulhun

2005–11 Zurich University of Teacher Education (PHZH). Didactics Researcher, People & Environment

1996–2001 Beige Swiss Styling. Co-founder and joint Managing Director

1988–2005 Canton of Zurich public schools. Class teacher teaching design, language, people & environment and sport

Publications (selection)

2023 *Leisten wir einander Gesellschaft?*, in: Beat Frank, *Skulpturen anwenden im Leben*, edition clandestin.
Architektur als Klassengesellschaft, in: *Arch+*.
Cara Mamma, in: *trans: journal of the Department of Architecture, ETH Zurich*

2022 *Give us a break! Arbeitermilieu und Designszene im Aufbruch*, Diaphanes.
Versteckte Täter:innen, in: *Widerspruch*

2021 *Les fleurs du bien – Wenn Diversität Gestalt annimmt*, in: *Differenz und Repräsentation*, Folkwang University of the Arts, edition assemblage.
Jugend und ihre Grenzen der Kreativität, in: *Widerspruch*.
Breaking Class – Upward Climbers and the Swiss Nature of Design History, in: *Swiss Design Network SDN*, Valiz

2020 Review: *Kolonialität und Geschlecht im 20. Jahrhundert* (Patricia Purtschert), Gender Campus blog.
Brennende Unschärfe and *Per arrivare bisogna partire*, in: *INES Handbuch Neue Schweiz*, Diaphanes

2019 *Quite Natural*, in: *trans magazin: journal of the Department of Architecture, ETH Zurich*.
Der Balken in meinem Auge: There's an Elephant in the Room, Zollfreilager/Theaterspektakel

2017 *Critical knitting*, in: *trans magazin: journal of the Department of Architecture, ETH Zurich*.
A double-quoted world, Art.School.Differences, ZHdK

Seminars and lectures 2010–23 (selection)

gta Institute, ETH Zurich:
Class Matters – in Architecture, Design and Art

ZHdK, Design Departement:
How Afropean is Switzerland? (Class Matters).
Modernism and Race.
Origin (Re)counts.
The Design of Social Climbing.
Design in a Social and Economic Context

ZHdK, Cultural Analysis Department:
Interculturality and Cultural Capital.
Processes for Assessing the Foreign from the Perspective of Social and Economic History.
Introduction to Scientific Reading

Lucerne University of Applied Sciences and Arts, Lucerne School of Design, Film and Art:
Social and Economic History of Textile Techniques and Materials.
Design History I and *Design History II.*
Introduction to Product Language: The Grammar of Collecting Textiles.
Economic, Environmental and Social Sustainability in the Textile Industry

Panel discussions, symposiums and conferences

2023 *Versteckte Täter:innen – Angriff auf Familien*, podium series by *Widerspruch* magazine.
Classism and Design, Futuress
2022 *Racialized Subjectivities* at the conference *Race and Racism – Putting Switzerland on the Map*, University of Fribourg
2021 Book launch, INES, *Handbuch Neue Schweiz*, Zurich
2019 *Ästhetik der Anpassung*, public symposium, host together with Prof. P. Ursprung, gta Institute, ETH Zurich, Zurich
2014 *Willy Guhl and the Look of Swiss Neutrality*, DHS Conference, Oxford University, UK
2013 *Provincializing Modernism*, DHS Conference, Ahmedabad, India

Performances with the Schwarzenbach-Komplex collective (selection)

T-Wort Performance and *Liebe Mobiliar…*, in: *Not the same procedure! Abend der Appelle*, at the Zürcher Theaterspektakel 2021.
Die Internationale ist eine nächtliche Weberin, in: *Abend der Appelle Basel*, INES-Tour de nouvelle Suisse, Kaserne Basel, 2022

Podcasts, broadcasts, radio plays (selection)

2023 SRF2 Kultur, *Soziale Herkunft und Design: Paola De Martins Recherche.*
Rosa Luxemburg Foundation, Manypod series, *Zerrissene Familien. Widerstand der Schweizer Secondos*
2022 Bayerischer Rundfunk co-production with Radio SRF2 Kultur, *Welcher Art die Wärme ist*, radio play, co-author with M. Nadj Abonji, C. Andreotti, directed by E. Altorfer, music by M. Schütz. Winner of Radio Play of the Month, October 2022
2021 SRF2 Kultur, *Saisonnierstatut: Das war ein Attentat auf die Familien*

Gran Premio svizzero di design 2024

Il Gran Premio svizzero di design omaggia carriere esemplari e offre visibilità a designer il cui lavoro apre prospettive o riflessioni particolarmente interessanti in questo campo.

Quali voci far sentire in un mondo così rumoroso come il nostro? Bisogna valorizzare coloro che generano idee per rendere più belli i nostri oggetti, i nostri manifesti, i nostri siti Internet e i nostri vestiti? Oppure coloro che li rendono più sostenibili? O forse va premiato chi vede nel design un atto sociale? Questa disciplina può essere portatrice di nuovi messaggi? Cosa significa, nel 2024, pensare e creare tenendo conto della diversità e della complessità del nostro mondo?

La giuria discute intensamente di questi temi e valuta con la massima attenzione il messaggio che intende trasmettere con l'attribuzione dei tre premi. Il suo intento è sempre quello di mettere in evidenza il lavoro di singoli individui che si distinguono per il loro approccio innovativo, creativo o impegnato oppure hanno influenzato o influenzano ancora in modo significativo la loro disciplina. E questo senza dimenticare le donne, che in passato hanno ricevuto poca visibilità. L'annuncio dei Gran Premi attira l'attenzione dei media e consente di far conoscere i diversi ambiti del design a un pubblico diversificato, ma non solo: il riconoscimento federale, conferito da pari, rende anche omaggio a professionisti e professioniste che esplorano i confini della propria pratica.

Nel 2024 sono state scelte persone che hanno intrapreso un percorso innovativo nel loro campo. Il contributo di Paola De Martin va ben oltre la ricerca tradizionale. Le sue riflessioni critiche guardano al design con un approccio transdisciplinare che si colloca in un determinato contesto sociale e politico e affronta questioni come la migrazione, il razzismo e l'esclusione sociale. La stilista Lucie Meier è protagonista di una carriera straordinaria: a soli 40 anni ha già lavorato per importanti case di moda come Louis Vuitton, Balenciaga, Dior et Jil Sander. Chi costruisce il proprio percorso professionale all'estero deve spesso attendere molto tempo prima che il suo operato venga riconosciuto in Svizzera. Il premio a Lucie Meier valorizza una designer che conosce nel profondo la propria disciplina. Infine, con i suoi 74 anni, Luciano Rigolini è un creatore che non ha mai smesso di interrogare le immagini. Esplora la sua materia facendola propria e si interessa in particolare alla fotografia vernacolare. Attraverso il suo sguardo, le fotografie rivelano nuove potenzialità plastiche. Tutto questo avviene in parallelo a una carriera internazionale comme produttore nel cinema documentario d'autore.

Riunendo sotto l'egida del Gran Premio svizzero di design 2024 tre personalità che si trovano in momenti diversi del loro percorso professionale e perseguono ognuna un approccio del tutto singolare, la giuria mostra che il

design apre molteplici prospettive. Riconoscere il lavoro di Paola De Martin, Lucie Meier e Luciano Rigolini, attivi in ambiti relativamente distanti fra loro, significa proprio questo. Le loro storie personali sono la prova che non è necessario appartenere a un'élite per aspirare al riconoscimento del proprio operato, perché gli elementi propulsori della loro creatività sono la riflessione e l'impegno.

Nathalie Herschdorfer, Presidente della Commissione federale del design

Prefazione

A 18 anni dal lancio, il Gran Premio svizzero di Design dell'Ufficio federale della cultura (UFC), il più alto riconoscimento per il design in Svizzera, continua a essere uno strumento eccezionale per mettere in luce le molteplici espressioni del design e la varietà degli sviluppi professionali in questo campo. Grazie alla valorizzazione di prospettive e approcci diversi, il nostro sguardo sull'importanza del design nella società diventa ogni anno più ricco e dinamico.

La prima edizione del Gran Premio svizzero di design si è tenuta nel 2007. Poco tempo prima l'UFC aveva abbandonato lo strumento dei contributi ai progetti di design e la Commissione federale del design (CFD) era alla ricerca di nuove possibilità per fornire a chi un sostegno finanziario mirato e proattivo alle eccellenze nel design.

Il primo anno, su proposta della CFD, sono stati assegnati cinque premi del valore di 40 000 franchi ciascuno. Due sono andati a personalità di fama internazionale: Adrian Frutiger, importante creatore di caratteri tipografici, e Bernhard Schobinger, uno dei più influenti designer di gioielli in Europa. Gli altri tre, invece, hanno voluto essere un riconoscimento alla generazione emergente e sono stati attribuiti all'agenzia Nose, fondata nel 1991, alla stilista Ruth Grüninger e al grafico Cornel Windlin, allora poco più che quarantenne. L'obiettivo dell'UFC era consentire a designer di talento di dedicarsi a progetti innovativi e sviluppare il loro potenziale creativo senza doversi concentrare esclusivamente sul successo commerciale.

I premi hanno segnato un pezzo di storia del design svizzero. La pubblicazione contiene spesso primi elementi d'archivio che poi serviranno come base per future presentazioni delle creazioni e per la ricerca. Proprio l'anno scorso si sono accesi i riflettore su diversi vincitori e vincitrici delle edizioni precedenti del Gran Premio svizzero di design: il Museo nazionale svizzero ha allestito una mostra monografica sull'eccezionale talento della stilista Ursula Rodel (premiata nel 2009); a settembre è stato pubblicato un catalogo completo dei lavori di Rosmarie Baltensweiler (premiata nel 2019), visionaria designer di lampade; Eleonore Peduzzi Riva (premiata nel 2023), l'architetta e designer che ha contribuito a sviluppare il celebre divano DS 600 e molto altro ancora, è stata più volte intervistata e invitata a partecipare a tavole rotonde; il Museum für Gestaltung di Zurigo ha esposto recentemente i magnifici tessuti di Claudia Caviezel (premiata nel 2016); Sarah Kueng e Lovis Caputo (premiate nel 2020) hanno ricevuto il meritato Goldene Hase della rivista Hochparterre, e la casa editrice About Books sta per pubblicare un volume con 12 nuovi tipi di carattere ideati da Rosmarie Tissi (premiata nel 2018).

Le vincitrici e il vincitore di quest'anno, Paola De Martin, Lucie Meier e Luciano Rigolini, hanno in comune la capacità di mettere in discussione le tradizioni e percorrere nuove strade. Con il loro approccio innovativo contribuiscono a promuovere la diversità, l'inclusione, l'etica, la collaborazione e la tecnologia nella cultura. Scoprite come tra le pagine di questa pubblicazione, che spero possa essere ricca di spunti interessanti e, come ogni anno, fonte di ispirazione per i vostri progetti futuri.

Anna Niederhäuser
Responsabile di design
Ufficio federale della cultura

Swiss Grand Award for Design 2024

The Swiss Grand Award for Design honours outstanding careers and casts a spotlight on creators whose work breaks new ground or explores interesting new intellectual avenues in this domain.

Which voices should we allow to be heard amidst the clamour of our world? Should we favour those whose creativity makes our objects, posters, websites or clothes more beautiful? What about those who make them more sustainable, or those who view design as a social practice? Can design convey new messages? What, in 2024, does it mean to think and create while acknowledging the diversity and complexity of our world?

The Jury engages in vigorous debate on these questions and pays a great deal of attention to the message it wishes to send out with its choice of three winners. It wants to showcase individuals with particularly innovative, creative or activist approaches as well as those that have influenced or continue to influence their discipline in a significant way – without forgetting women, of course, who were less visible in the past especially. The announcement of the Grand Award winners attracts media attention and gives the various design disciplines exposure to a broader public. An award sponsored by the federal government and handed out by peers is also a way of paying tribute to professionals who push the envelope in their chosen field and leave their mark on it through innovation, creativity or activism.

For 2024, we have chosen three innovators. Paola De Martin's work goes way beyond traditional research. She takes a critical view and a transdisciplinary approach to design, embedding it in a sociopolitical context by relating it to issues of migration, racism and social exclusion. The fashion designer Lucie Meier has had an enviable international career to date. Still only 40, she has worked for some of the great fashion houses, including Louis Vuitton, Balenciaga, Dior and Jil Sander. Recognition in Switzerland often comes late to those who pursue a career abroad, but Lucie Meier deserves this award due to her excellent, nuanced mastery of her craft. For his part, 74-year-old Luciano Rigolini has never tired of questioning images. He explores his material through appropriation, taking a particularly keen interest in vernacular photography and unlocking new dimensions of sculpturally. At the same time, he has pursued an international as a producer in auteur documentary films.

In selecting three individuals at different stages in their professional lives for the Swiss Grand Award for Design 2024, each with their own unique approach, the Jury highlights the variety of perspectives design can open up. The practices of Paola De Martin, Lucie Meier and Luciano Rigolini have relatively little in common and thus demonstrate the many career paths designers are free to choose. Their personal stories make it clear that

recognition does not hinge on being part of an elite: it can come through considered, committed creativity.

Nathalie Herschdorfer, Chair of the Federal Design Commission

Introduction

Even 18 years after the Swiss Grand Award for Design was launched, this highest honour for Swiss designers remains an outstanding instrument for the Federal Office of Culture (FOC) to showcase the wide range of potential career paths and the diversity of the design field. As we recognise a variety of different perspectives and approaches, our understanding of the importance of design for society as a whole is enriched and enlivened year by year.

The Grand Award was first presented in 2007. At that time, the FOC had recently discontinued its design project subsidies, and the Federal Design Commission was looking for new, more targeted and proactive ways to support designers with funding.

Five awards worth CHF 40,000 each were handed out in the first year at the Commission's suggestion. The winners included two internationally renowned personalities: the type designer Adrian Frutiger and Bernhard Schobinger, one of Europe's most influential jewellery artists. At the same time, the younger generation was represented by the design agency Nose, founded in 1991, as well as fashion designer Ruth Grüninger and graphic artist Cornel Windlin, who had only just turned 40. The FOC's aim was to enable design practitioners to work on innovative projects and develop their creative potential without having to focus solely on commercial success.

The Grand Award encapsulates a piece of Swiss design history. The accompanying publication often contains previously unseen archive pictures and serves as a basis for future work presentations and research projects. Just last year, a number of former winners were back in the spotlight. The Swiss National Museum hosted a monographic exhibition of the exceptionally talented Swiss fashion designer Ursula Rodel (Grand Award winner in 2009). An extensive catalogue of works by lighting design pioneer Rosmarie Baltensweiler (winner in 2019) was published in September. Eleonore Peduzzi Riva (winner in 2023), who had a hand in far more than just the world-famous DS-600 sofa, was invited to a number of panels and interviews. Zurich's Museum für Gestaltung presented the wonderful textile works of Claudia Caviezel (winner in 2016), while at the end of the year, Sarah Kueng and Lovis Caputo (winners in 2020) received a well-deserved Golden Hare award from *Hochparterre* magazine. We are also delighted to see a brand-new work by Rosmarie Tissi (winner in 2018), comprising 12 new alphabets, published by About Books.

This year's winners – Paola De Martin, Lucie Meier and Luciano Rigolini – are all trailblazers who have succeeded in questioning traditions. Read on to find out how their groundbreaking work has promoted diversity, inclusion, ethics, cooperation and technology in cultural circles. I hope you find their stories fascinating and, like every year, take inspiration from them for your own projects.

Anna Niederhäuser
Head of Design
Federal Office of Culture

[DE → p. 3, FR → p. 5]

Swiss Grand Award for Design Winners 2007–24

2024
Paola De Martin
  Designer and design researcher
Lucie Meier
  Fashion designer and creative director
Luciano Rigolini
  Photographer and producer for auteur documentary films

2023
Etienne Delessert
  Illustrator and graphic designer
Eleonore Peduzzi Riva
  Interior architect and consultant
Chantal Prod'Hom
  Museum director and curator

2022
Susanne Bartsch
  Talent curator and event producer
Verena Huber
  Interior architect
Beat Streuli
  Artist

2021
Julia Born
  Graphic designer
Peter Knapp
  Photographer and art director
Sarah Owens
  Design educator and researcher

2020
Ida Gut
  Fashion designer
Monique Jacot
  Photographer
Kueng Caputo
  Product designers

2019
Rosmarie Baltensweiler
  Product designer
Connie Hüsser
  Interior stylist
Thomi Wolfensberger
  Lithographer and publisher

2018
Cécile Feilchenfeldt
  Textile designer
Felco
  Product design
Rosmarie Tissi
  Graphic designer

2017
David Bielander
  Jewellery designer
Thomas Ott
  Illustrator
Jean Widmer
  Graphic designer and art director

2016
Claudia Caviezel
  Textile designer
Hans Eichenberger
  Product and interior designer
Ralph Schraivogel
  Graphic designer

2015
Luc Chessex
  Photographer
Lora Lamm
  Graphic designer
Team '77
  Typographers and type designers

2014
Erich Biehle
  Textile designer
Alfredo Häberli
  Furniture and product designer
Wolfgang Weingart
  Typographer

2013
Trix & Robert Haussmann
  Interior and product designers
Armin Hofmann
  Graphic designer
Martin Leuthold
  Textile designer

2012
Franco Clivio
  Product designer
Gavillet & Rust
  Graphic designers
Karl Gerstner
  Graphic designer

2011
Jörg Boner
  Product designer
NORM
  Graphic designers
Ernst Scheidegger
  Photographer
Walter Steiger
  Footwear designer

2010
Susi & Ueli Berger
  Furniture designers
Jean-Luc Godard
  Filmmaker
Sonnhild Kestler
  Textile designer
Otto Künzli
  Jewellery designer

2009
Robert Frank
  Photographer
Christoph Hefti
  Textile designer
Ursula Rodel
  Fashion designer
Thut Möbel
  Furniture design

2008
Holzer Kobler Architekturen
  Exhibition designers and architects
Albert Kriemler (Akris)
  Fashion designer
Alain Kupper
  Graphic designer, musician and artist
Walter Pfeiffer
  Photographer

2007
Ruth Grüninger
  Fashion designer
NOSE
  Communication design, service design
Bernhard Schobinger
  Jewellery designer
Adrian Frutiger
  Type desinger
Cornel Windlin
  Graphic designer

Swiss Federal Design Commission 2024

Chair
Nathalie Herschdorfer
  Director, Photo Élysée

Members
Cécile Feilchenfeldt
  Textile designer, Paris
Davide Fornari
  Professor for Research and Development at ECAL, Renens
David Glättli
  Industrial designer and creative director, Zurich/ Tokyo
Andreas Gysin
  Programmer and graphic designer, Lugano
Vera Sacchetti
  Design critic and curator, Basel
Ivan Sterzinger
  Graphic designer and publisher, Zurich

Colophon

Published on the occasion of the Swiss Grand Award for Design 2024

Head of project
  Anna Niederhäuser
  Federal Office of Culture (FOC), Bern

Editing, project coordination
  Mirjam Fischer
  mille pages, Zurich

Art direction and design
  Guillaume Chuard
  (Studio Ardworks),
  Lausanne / London

Typeface
  LL Geigy,
  Robert Huber / Lineto, Zurich

Photography (p. 7)
  © FOC / Diana Pfammatter

Translations
  Aurélie Duthoo (DE → FR)
  Silvia Giacomotti (DE/FR → IT)
  Lucas Moreno (IT → FR)
  Philippe Moser (FR / IT → DE)
  Mark O'Neil (FR → EN)
  Alain Perrinjaquet (DE → FR)
  Sarah Ponting (IT → EN)
  Annie Urselli (DE → IT)

Proofreading
  FOC Translation Services (DE / FR / IT)
  Mark O'Neil (EN)

Printing
  Gremper AG, Basel

Weitere Übersetzungen der Gespräche finden Sie auf:
Veuillez trouver les traductions françaises sur:
La traduzione italiana delle interviste è disponibile su:
www.schweizerkulturpreise.ch/design

© 2024 Federal Office of Culture, Bern and Verlag Scheidegger & Spiess AG, Zurich

Texts © the authors
Images © the artists

Verlag Scheidegger & Spiess
Niederdorfstrasse 54
8001 Zurich, Switzerland
www.scheidegger-spiess.ch

Scheidegger & Spiess is being supported by the Federal Office of Culture with a general subsidy for the years 2021–24.

All rights reserved; no part of this publication may be reproduced, stored in a retrieval system or transmitted in any form or by any means, electronic, mechanical, photocopying, recording, or otherwise, without the prior written consent of the publisher.

The three winners of the Swiss Grand Award for Design 2024 are: Paola De Martin, designer and design researcher, Lucie Meier, fashion designer and creative director, Luciano Rigolini, photographer and producer for auteur documentary film. The publication is distributed in a box containing three individual booklets – one for each winner – that are not available separately.

ISBN: 978-3-03942-207-4

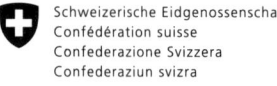

Schweizerische Eidgenossenschaft
Confédération suisse
Confederazione Svizzera
Confederaziun svizra

Eidgenössisches Departement des Innern EDI
Département fédéral de l'intérieur DFI
Dipartimento federale dell'interno DFI
Departament federal da l'intern DFI
Bundesamt für Kultur BAK
Office fédéral de la culture OFC
Ufficio federale della cultura UFC
Uffizi federal da cultura UFC